Diving & Snorkeling

Bahamas

Michael Lawrence

LONE   ATIONS
Melbo   on • Paris

Diving & Snorkeling Bahamas
- A Lonely Planet Pisces Book

1st Edition – May 2001

Published by
Lonely Planet Publications
90 Maribyrnong St., Footscray, Victoria 3011, Australia

Other offices
150 Linden Street, Oakland, California 94607, USA
10a Spring Place, London NW5 3BH, UK
1 rue du Dahomey, 75011 Paris, France

Photographs
All photographs, including covers, by Michael Lawrence

Front cover photograph
Snorkeler with cushion sea stars, Marsh Harbour, Abacos

Back cover photographs
Queen conch
Divers kneeling at Shark Wall, New Providence
Footprints and snorkel gear on beach, Exumas

All of the images in this guide are available for
    licensing from **Lonely Planet Images**
email: lpi@lonelyplanet.com.au

ISBN 1 86450 181 2

text & maps © Lonely Planet 2001
photographs © photographers as indicated 2001
dive site maps are Transverse Mercator projection

LONELY PLANET and the Lonely Planet logo are
trademarks of Lonely Planet Publications Pty Ltd.

Printed by H&Y Printing Ltd., Hong Kong

Contents

New Providence Dive Sites   42

Grand Bahama Dive Sites   57

Bimini Dive Sites   72

Berry Islands Dive Sites   86

Authors

ROB WATERFIELD

Michael Lawrence

Michael Lawrence's life has been a twisting, turning path of wildly divergent careers. He was a professional musician for nearly 25 years, playing jazz guitar, doing studio work, orchestral work, stage shows, arranging and conducting and doing anything possible to turn jazz pennies into real dollars. A gig on a cruise ship in the Caribbean allowed him his first opportunity to view the underwater world, an experience that soon changed his life. A highly regarded marine photojournalist, Michael has written and illustrated well over 350 articles for virtually every North American dive publication as well as various publications in South America and Europe. His photos, both underwater and topside, have been published internationally in magazines, calendars, textbooks and advertisements for a variety of industries. Michael currently lives landlocked in Indiana with his new wife, two children, two cats and a huge iguana. He is also the author of the Lonely Planet Pisces *Diving & Snorkeling Dominica*.

From the Author

After two decades diving The Bahamas, it is virtually impossible to thank everyone who has made this author's work possible. I offer my apologies, love and affection to anyone not included in this regrettably short list: First, to my close friend Neal Watson, Bahamas pioneer and holder of multiple world diving records: thanks for your unflagging friendship and support. Caroline Courtney: thank you for years of companionship, guidance, superb modeling and honest warmth. To Carolyn Pascal-Gaurino and Paul Tzimoulis: thanks for so many valuable assignments. You opened the door to the country. To the following, thank you for dive support, shared meals, conversation and laughter: Stuart and Michelle Cove; Maura Brassil of the Out Islands Promotion Board; Gary and Brenda Adkison and Barry Albury of Walker's Cay; Ollie Ferguson and John Englander from UNEXSO; the folks at Xanadu on Grand Bahama; the entire Birch family from Small Hope Bay; Bill and Nowdla Keefe of Bimini Undersea; Frazier Nivens and Gene Kruger of Nassau Scuba Centre; Jef Fox; Bill Whiteland of Bahama Divers; Jorge Friese, Peter Kuska and the whole gang at Stella Maris on Long Island; Riding Rock Inn on San Salvador; Skeet LaChance and Nekton Diving Cruises.

Photography Notes

Michael Lawrences uses Nikon Cameras for both underwater and land shooting. Underwater he uses Nikon 8008s, N90s and F4 cameras in Aquatica housings, using 16mm, 18mm and 35mm lenses and various extension tubes for some of his macro work. His strobes of choice are Ikelite 150s and 200s. On land he uses Nikon N90s and F5 cameras with a full array of lenses. The vast majority of images in this volume were shot of Fuji Velvia and Provia, but he also carries Kodachrome 25 and 64 (when there's time to wait for processing), Ektachrome 100SW and Ektachrome 200SW for low-light situations.

From the Publisher

This first edition was produced in Lonely Planet's U.S. office under direction from Roslyn Bullas, the Pisces Books publishing manager. Wendy Smith edited the book, with invaluable contributions from fellow editor David Lauterborn. Christine Lee floated in to proofread in the final stages. Emily Douglas designed the book's content and cover. Sara Nelson, John Spelman, Colin Bishop, Eric Thomsen, Ivy Feibelman and Kat Smith created the maps under the supervision of U.S. Cartography Manager Alex Guilbert.

Pisces Pre-Dive Safety Guidelines

Before embarking on a scuba diving, skin diving or snorkeling trip, carefully consider the following to help ensure a safe and enjoyable experience:

- Possess a current diving certification card from a recognized scuba diving instructional agency (if scuba diving)
- Be sure you are healthy and feel comfortable diving
- Obtain reliable information about physical and environmental conditions at the dive site (e.g., from a reputable local dive operation)
- Be aware of local laws, regulations and etiquette about marine life and environment
- Dive at sites within your experience level; if possible, engage the services of a competent, professionally trained dive instructor or divemaster

Underwater conditions vary significantly from one region, or even site, to another. Seasonal changes can significantly alter site and dive conditions. These differences influence the way divers dress for a dive and what diving techniques they use.

There are special requirements for diving in any area, regardless of location. Before your dive, ask about environmental characteristics that can affect your diving and how trained local divers deal with these considerations.

Warning & Request

Things change—dive site conditions, regulations, topside information. Nothing stays the same for long. Your feedback on this book will be used to help update and improve the next edition. Excerpts from your correspondence may appear in *Planet Talk*, our quarterly newsletter, or *Comet*, our monthly email newsletter. Please let us know if you do not want your letter published or your name acknowledged.

Correspondence can be addressed to:
Lonely Planet Publications
Pisces Books
150 Linden Street
Oakland, CA 94607
email: pisces@lonelyplanet.com

Introduction

With more than 700 islands and cays strewn across 100,000 sq miles (259,000 sq km) of transparent blue tropical seas, The Bahamas has drawn divers to its shores since the very inception of international dive travel. Impressions of the country are easily dominated by images of the sea. Huge expanses of swirling, shallow sand flats lend the water a sparkling turquoise hue, giving way abruptly to the breathtakingly rich, cobalt blue of the deep abyss.

Many people mistakenly believe The Bahamas lie within the Caribbean Sea. In truth the archipelago rests in the western central Atlantic, north of Cuba. As a result, the area shares some of the best features of the Caribbean combined with the rich marine life of the Atlantic. With virtually no runoff, sedimentation is minimal, creating tropical waters with a crystalline clarity rivaling any on the planet.

Within the country's boundaries, divers can access one of the most extensive and varied rosters of dive experiences available in this hemisphere. Lush shallow coral reefs, vertical walls dripping with sponges and gorgonians, a healthy population of

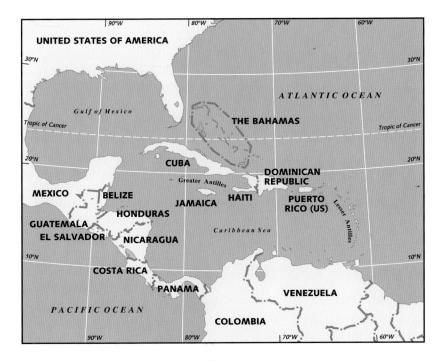

tropical and pelagic fish, modern and historic wrecks, labyrinthine tunnels and caverns, blue holes leading to elaborate submerged cave systems, encounters with sharks and dolphins—the impressive list goes on and on.

Because of its proximity to the United States, The Bahamas has long been a popular getaway, not just for divers but also for beachgoers, fishing enthusiasts and other lovers of the ocean. With its tropical culture, English-speaking population, ready acceptance of U.S. currency and generally friendly attitude, The Bahamas is an easy culture for visitors to feel comfortable in.

Early inhabitants came from diverse backgrounds—many were ex-slaves, expatriate British Loyalists and honest seafaring folk, while some came from more nefarious backgrounds, adding to the vivid tapestry of Bahamian culture. Of a total population numbering about 290,000, nearly 200,000 live in the Nassau area on New Providence. Another 50,000 live on Grand Bahama, and the rest are spread across another two dozen or so populated islands. Nassau, the country's capital, offers the bustling aura of a real city. You can find the same sense of excitement, though to a lesser degree, in Grand Bahama's Freeport/Port Lucaya area. Both islands have their quiet sides outside the tourist-oriented areas, especially Grand Bahama, where you'll find tranquil towns and vast unoccupied tracts of land.

The rest of the country stands in marked contrast to these two more-urban areas. The other islands in the archipelago are known as the Family Islands or, more traditionally, the Out Islands. These far-flung places offer pristine beaches covered in fine white sand, alternating with areas of rough, pockmarked limestone known as ironshore. Locals live in small settlements or isolated homes along the shore. There are a few larger towns, some of them very quaint and charming.

Though just a tiny fraction of the perhaps thousands of diveable spots in The Bahamas, the 108 dive sites covered in this book represent the best and most popular sites throughout the country. Information about location, depth range, access

and expertise rating is provided for each site. You'll also find detailed descriptions of each site, outlining conditions, topographic features and the types of marine life you can expect to see. The Marine Life section provides a gallery of The Bahamas' common fish and invertebrate life. Though this book is not meant to be a stand-alone travel guidebook, the Practicalities and Overview sections offer useful information about the islands, and the Activities & Attractions section provides ideas about how to spend your time out of the water.

Overview

With its westernmost islands only 48 miles (77km) off the Florida coastline, The Bahamas stretches southeast for more than 750 miles (1,200km), extending past Cuba and ending off Hispaniola. The country's more than 100,000 sq miles (259,000 sq km) of water area dwarfs its 5,382 sq miles (13,939 sq km) of landmass. The country is made up of about 25 main islands or island groups, more than 650 cays (pronounced "keys") and some 2,400 islets and exposed rocks. It is a notably low-lying country—the average height of the islands is no more than 45ft (14m) above sea level, and its highest point reaches a towering 206ft (63m).

History

October 12, 1992, marked the 500th anniversary of the "discovery" of the Americas by Christopher Columbus. While there is no doubt that the islands of The Bahamas were the first of the New World spotted by Columbus, debate continues over the exact location of his first landfall. For years the island now called San Salvador was accorded this honor, but Long Island also vies for this recognition—both islands boast monuments to the occasion.

When Columbus arrived, he was greeted by the Lucayans (from the native *lukku-cairi*, or "island people"), descendants of the South American Arawak Indians. These peaceful people had migrated to the Caribbean and then north to The Bahamas around the 6th or 7th centuries to escape the attacks of the warlike Carib Indians.

The Bahamas did not hold the treasure that Columbus sought, and he moved on after naming the area La Baja Mar, Spanish for "the low (or shallow) sea." Spanish settlers enslaved the Lucayans to work the mines of Hispaniola and Cuba. Decimated by disease and overwork, the Lucayan nation was virtually exterminated within a single generation. Their culture survives only in a few rare artifacts, petroglyphs and stone carvings. Pieces of their language also survive—tobacco, avocado, iguana, guava, hurricane, manatee, canoe, cay, hammock and barbecue are just a few words with Lucayan roots.

After the depopulation of the islands, The Bahamas lay uncolonized for nearly a century, attracting mainly shipwrecked sailors, beachcombers and pirates. Piracy, rum-running and wrecking (drawing unwary ships onto dangerous shoals to plunder their cargo) are part and parcel of the history and mystique of The Bahamas. Tales of famous pirates and the hidden treasures they left behind are traded throughout the islands to this day.

Early colonists included the Eleutherian Adventurers, a group of Bermudians seeking religious and cultural freedom from the British Crown in the mid-1600s. After the American Revolution, Loyalists (American colonists still loyal to the British) colonized much of The Bahamas. The Crown provided aid to its subjects in the form of transportation, land grants and supplies. In a five-year span during the late 18th century the population of The Bahamas tripled, reaching a whopping 10,000 citizens.

Columbus monument.

During the colonial era, plantations throughout the New World were worked by African slaves—men, women and children who came largely from West African tribes. Despite the influx of people and resources, attempts to establish a prosperous plantation economy were frustrated by the thin, easily exhausted topsoil. With the abolition of slavery in the mid-1800s, many settlers returned to Europe. Though Bahamian slavery never reached the proportions it did in other Caribbean nations, the institution had a marked impact on the people and culture of this nation. Some 85% of today's population is of African descent, and African traditions form an important part of Bahamian life.

Tourism first came to The Bahamas toward the end of the 19th century—1873 saw 500 winter visitors to Nassau, a banner year. From these humble beginnings the tourism industry has grown to become a mainstay of the Bahamian gross national product. The Bahamas expects to greet some 4 million visitors a year at the start of the 21st century.

Geography

The Bahamas owes its very existence to the sea and its creatures. The banks and islands are formed of millions of bead-shaped oolites, the skeletal remains of ocean creatures. Over eons, layer upon layer of these remains formed a limestone base more than 20,000ft (6,100m) thick. The islands are coral structures sprouting from this base.

Most of the islands sit on the outside edges of several large, barely submerged plateaus known as the Bahama Banks. All in all, there are some 20 separate platforms and pinnacles awash in water seldom deeper than 20ft (6.1m). These plateaus are separated by deep oceanic trenches, including the Tongue of the Ocean, the Exuma Sound and the Providence Channels, which drop precipitously to extreme depths. The Bahamian archipelago also includes several islands to the south and east that are the isolated peaks of undersea pinnacles. These include wall-diving legends such as San Salvador, Rum Cay and Conception Island, as well as a smattering of lesser-known islands and cays.

During the last Ice Age, when water levels in this region receded by as much as 400ft, the banks stood as high and dry as the flat-topped mesas of the American Southwest, surrounded by vertigo-inducing vertical cliffs. The deep-water trenches would have formed a network of massive saltwater rivers and bays running between the various plateaus and around the mountain peaks. Today these cliffs provide hundreds of miles of awe-inspiring drop-offs and walls.

The ledges along the drop-offs are evidence of the changing sea levels throughout geologic history—each represents an ancient shoreline during a pause in the rising of the seas. Generally speaking, there is a sand ledge at 80ft (24m), another sloping ledge at 120 to 140ft (37 to 43m) and yet another at around 200ft (61m).

Further evidence of the sea-level changes can be seen in the maze of caverns, tunnels and caves that honeycombs the limestone platforms. The stalactites and stalagmites inside some of these structures were formed when the caves were filled with air rather than water.

Blue Holes

The limestone platforms of The Bahamas are peppered with blue holes, perhaps more than any other destination in the world. The holes are the result of changing sea levels (the seas were much lower 10,000 years ago) and chemical reactions (the combination of fresh water and carbon dioxide creates carbolic acid, which dissolves the limestone). The largest concentrations of blue holes are found around Cay Sal Bank, Andros, Grand Bahama and the Exumas, though you'll find many others throughout the country.

The classic blue hole has a circular opening as broad as 100ft (30m) and drops vertically, opening up into a bell shape inside. Some are inaccessible, and others have narrow fissures that open into surprisingly large rooms. Inside, the walls often exhibit small caverns, as well as ledges and shelves. Many blue holes lead into cavern systems, and series of blue holes are often interconnected in a honeycomb of tunnels that interlaces the country. Most bottom out around 300 to 350ft (91 to 107m), but may penetrate the earth's crust by as much as 650ft (198m) or more. Landlocked blue holes start at the surface, while oceanic ones may start just below the surface or deeper, opening into a stretch of flat seafloor or wall.

It is important to use good judgment when diving in and around blue holes. Unless you are cave-certified, you must stay within sight of the opening. The wise diver will seek orientation and training before entering even an easily accessible cavern. Especially beware of the boiling holes. These small blue holes are connected to the ocean and exhibit an extreme flow of water during tidal changes. The surface of the water actually bubbles on one tide and sucks water deep into the bowels of the earth on the return. Oddly, it's on the low tide that they boil—the drop of the waterline forces water through the system and out of the holes. It may be impossible to enter the hole during these periods. On a rising high tide, the hole sucks water into its mouth off the flats. This is the most dangerous time to dive, as it can be difficult to escape the flow. The clearest water is found on a slack low tide, while the lowest visibility is found during the slack high tide—just the opposite of ocean diving.

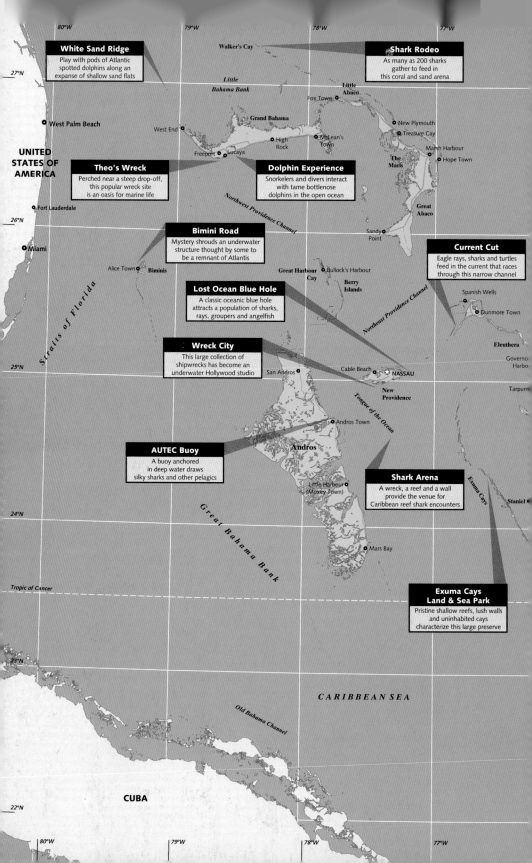

White Sand Ridge
Play with pods of Atlantic spotted dolphins along an expanse of shallow sand flats

Shark Rodeo
As many as 200 sharks gather to feed in this coral and sand arena

Theo's Wreck
Perched near a steep drop-off, this popular wreck site is an oasis for marine life

Dolphin Experience
Snorkelers and divers interact with tame bottlenose dolphins in the open ocean

Bimini Road
Mystery shrouds an underwater structure thought by some to be a remnant of Atlantis

Current Cut
Eagle rays, sharks and turtles feed in the current that races through this narrow channel

Lost Ocean Blue Hole
A classic oceanic blue hole attracts a population of sharks, rays, groupers and angelfish

Wreck City
This large collection of shipwrecks has become an underwater Hollywood studio

AUTEC Buoy
A buoy anchored in deep water draws silky sharks and other pelagics

Shark Arena
A wreck, a reef and a wall provide the venue for Caribbean reef shark encounters

Exuma Cays Land & Sea Park
Pristine shallow reefs, lush walls and uninhabited cays characterize this large preserve

27°N
26°N
25°N
24°N
23°N
22°N

80°W
79°W
78°W
77°W

Walker's Cay

Little Bahama Bank

Little Abaco
Fox Town

Grand Bahama

New Plymouth
Treasure Cay

West Palm Beach

West End
High Rock
McLean's Town
Freeport
Lucaya

Marsh Harbour
Hope Town

The Marls

UNITED STATES OF AMERICA

Northwest Providence Channel

Great Abaco

Fort Lauderdale

Sandy Point

Miami

Alice Town
Biminis

Great Harbour Cay
Bullock's Harbour

Spanish Wells

Berry Islands

Dunmore Town

Northeast Providence Channel

Eleuthera

Straits of Florida

San Andros
Cable Beach
NASSAU

Governo Harbo

Tarpun

New Providence

Andros Town

Tongue of the Ocean

Andros

Exuma Cays

Staniel

Little Harbour (Moxey Town)

Great Bahama Bank

Mars Bay

Tropic of Cancer

CARIBBEAN SEA

Old Bahama Channel

CUBA

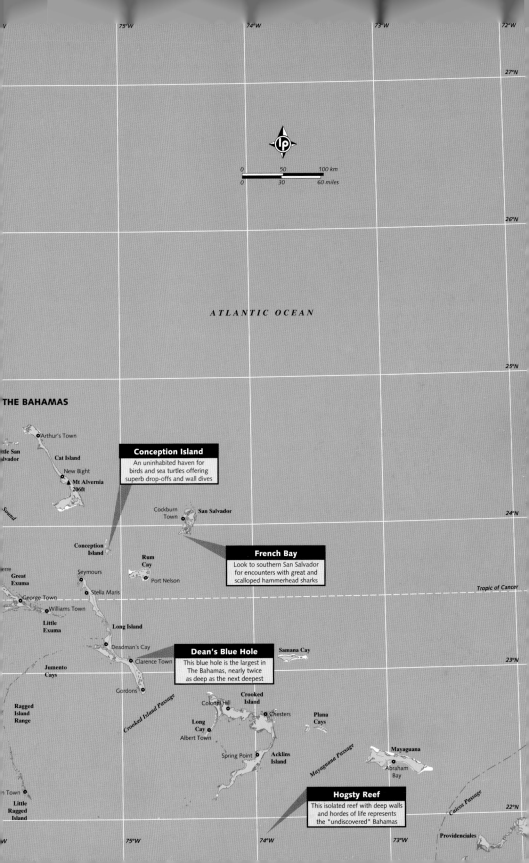

75°W 74°W 73°W 72°W

27°N

26°N

0   50   100 km
0   30   60 miles

ATLANTIC OCEAN

25°N

THE BAHAMAS

○Arthur's Town
ttle San
alvador   Cat Island
           New Bight
        ▲ Mt Alvernia
           206ft

Sound

Conception Island
An uninhabited haven for
birds and sea turtles offering
superb drop-offs and wall dives

Cockburn   ○San Salvador
Town   ○

24°N

Conception
Island ○

Rum
Cay ○

Port Nelson ○

French Bay
Look to southern San Salvador
for encounters with great and
scalloped hammerhead sharks

ierre
Great
Exuma   Seymours ○
        ○ Stella Maris

○George Town   *Tropic of Cancer*

○Williams Town

Little
Exuma   **Long Island**

                                        Samana Cay ○
        ○Deadman's Cay
        ○Clarence Town   **Dean's Blue Hole**   23°N
Jumento   This blue hole is the largest in
Cays   The Bahamas, nearly twice
                       as deep as the next deepest
        Gordons ○

Ragged
Island   Colonel Hill ○   **Crooked**
Range   **Island**
                                        ○ Chesters   Plana
                Long   Cays
                Cay ○
                Albert Town ○

        Spring Point ○   Acklins
                          Island   Mayaguana ○

                                                    Abraham
                                                    Bay ○

n Town ○   Celcos Passage   22°N
        Little   **Hogsty Reef**
        Ragged   This isolated reef with deep walls
        Island   and hordes of life represents
                         the "undiscovered" Bahamas

75°W   74°W   73°W   Providenciales ○

Practicalities

Climate

Sometimes referred to as "The Isles of Perpetual June," The Bahamas enjoy a near-ideal climate. Year-round warm temperatures are the rule, both in and out of the water. The Tropic of Cancer cuts through Long Island and Great Exuma, so The Bahamas are classified as both tropical and subtropical. In reality, the variation between the north and south of the archipelago is minimal. During summer (May through October), daytime temperatures average between 80 and 90°F (27 to 32°C). It cools off a bit in winter (November through April), but temperatures still average a balmy 70 to 80°F (21 to 27°C). The rainy season runs from late May to November, though some rain may fall at any time of the year.

Summer water temperatures range from a low of 78°F (26°C) to a high of 84°F (29°C). You won't need anything more than a diveskin or thin neoprene wetsuit. During the coolest months (December through March), water temperatures drop as low as 68°F (20°C) to a high of 76°F (24°C). At this time of year a 3 to 5mm wetsuit is recommended.

Hurricane season runs from late June through November. Hurricane season is not cause for great concern, but should be kept in mind, as hurricane activity has increased significantly since 1995.

Language

English is the official language of The Bahamas. Locals speak with a slight West Indian accent, and their vocabulary leans more toward British than American English.

Getting There

Commercial airlines service airports in both Nassau (on New Providence) and Freeport (on Grand Bahama) several times daily through gateway cities in the U.S. (Miami, Fort Lauderdale, West Palm Beach, Atlanta, Dallas, Charlotte, Philadelphia and New York), Canada (Montreal and Toronto) and Europe (London, Paris, Milan and Frankfurt).

There are also regularly scheduled direct flights to several of the Out Islands, including the Abacos, Bimini, Eleuthera, Great Exuma and San Salvador. Charter flights originate from at least two dozen other cities in the U.S., Canada and

Europe. Airline schedules change frequently, so the best way to explore the possibilities is to check with your dive-savvy travel agent, with your resort or simply to let your dive operator arrange a flight for you.

Private pilots have ready access to The Bahamas, as virtually every one of the Out Islands has an airstrip. At least a dozen islands also have customs and immigration agents to assist you. Entry is also easy for boaters coming from the U.S., who usually make landfall at Grand Bahama, Walker's Cay (northern Abacos), Bimini or Cat Cay (just south of Bimini).

Cruise ships call at the main ports in Nassau and Grand Bahama's West End nearly every day of the week. They often allow a week (or more) layover as part of a round-trip itinerary.

Gateway City – Nassau

Nassau, on the north side of New Providence Island, is The Bahamas' capital and seat of government. The city, in conjunction with Paradise Island just off the north coast, is known worldwide for its five-star hotels, casinos, beaches, golf courses and other tourism facilities. Nassau's fine natural harbor has it made a bustling center of shipping traffic. Its proximity to Miami has also helped to make it one of the most popular cruise ports in the world, welcoming more than 2.5 million passengers each year. The docks are capable of accommodating a dozen ships at a time, and any given day will find at least a few ships docked. Nassau may not be the prettiest town in The Bahamas, but it is historic and quaint in its own way. Visitors must remember that Nassau is the commercial center of The Bahamas, and a working waterfront is rarely attractive, no matter where you travel in the world. However, even on Bay Street (the street bordering the harbor) you can find numerous reminders of Nassau's old-time charm.

Connected to downtown Nassau by a bridge, Paradise Island (originally called Hog Island) has reached the saturation point of resort development. Although the island has been transformed forever, its natural beauty remains evident in its long strands of perfect beaches. As an upscale resort destination, Paradise

A quaint horse-drawn buggy adds to Nassau's charm.

Island is unbeatable. Another favored spot for tourists and locals alike is Cable Beach, just west of downtown Nassau. Cable Beach is a popular resort area replete with beaches, large hotels, a casino, shopping and restaurants.

Gateway City – Freeport

The second main town in The Bahamas is Freeport on Grand Bahama. This is an area of shopping, big hotels, casinos, marinas and general fun-in-the-sun activities. Much of the tourism activity is centered around Port Lucaya, which has large and recently refurbished hotels, a great shopping area, one of the oldest dive operations in The Bahamas and a superb marina. The beaches along this part of the southern shore are bustling with a full array of beach activities and watersports. The shopping area boasts internationally recognized retail names and a pile of great Bahamian and international restaurants ranging from elegant to funky. You can also choose from a handful of unique, personable bars.

Another noteworthy area is the Princess Casino complex. A hotel and casino, the Princess also includes the International Bazaar, an elaborate shopping area with bars, restaurants and shops of all sizes. The complex is divided into territories representing various nations—one alleyway has an Indian theme, another a Chinese theme, and so on. The complex's large straw market offers Bahamian and imported pseudo-Bahamian goods (mostly straw goods, hence the name). The Princess complex is about 15 minutes by car or taxi from the beach.

Getting Around

There are several ways to travel between the islands. Bahamasair (☎ 377-5505 or toll-free ☎ 800-222-4262), the national air carrier, serves Nassau and the main Out Islands. Unfortunately, the planes seldom depart on schedule—it's not a question of if your flight will leave on time, but rather how late it will be. Another disadvantage is that all flights go through Nassau, which can make interisland air travel expensive and inconvenient. An alternative is to contact a charter airline or one of a variety of other small interisland airlines.

Another interisland travel option is to take a mail boat. Mail boats are still the lifeline of the Out Islands, as they provide an inexpensive way to get around the country—as long as you can spare the extra time. The schedule and destinations change frequently—get the latest pricing and scheduling information from the Dockmaster's Office (☎ 393-1064) at Potter's Cay, Nassau.

Rental cars are readily available on Grand Bahama and New Providence and can also be found on several of the larger Out Islands. The staff at your hotel is usually best equipped to make rental car arrangements. To rent a car, you must be 17 or older and have a valid drivers license and a credit card. An international drivers license, available through AAA, is also recommended but is not required.

Visitors staying longer than three months must acquire a Bahamian drivers license. On the Out Islands, gas stations tend to be few and far between, so keep an eye on your gas gauge. Reflecting the island's British heritage, driving is done on the left side of the road. The vast majority of rental cars are left-hand drive, though there are some right-hand drive vehicles. Also, if you're not familiar with them, be especially careful at roundabouts. When entering a roundabout, yield to vehicles already circling.

Taxis are abundant and readily available on all inhabited islands. Taxi rates vary depending on the type of service required. Rates from hotels to the airport are often higher than an equivalent on-island distance, and there may be additional charges for baggage and extra passengers. Taxi drivers tend to be honest about fares, but there is inevitably some variation in the rates charged. Though rare, metered cabs may be the best bet. You can also check the proper range of fares prior to your arrival. It's also possible for a family or small group to engage the services of a taxi driver for an informal tour of a given island.

Entry

Citizens of the U.S. and Canada may enter with proof of citizenship, such as a voter registration card, naturalization papers or a birth certificate, in conjunction with a photo ID. A passport is the simplest and best documentation to carry. Passports expired for less than five years may also be used.

Citizens of countries other than the U.S. and Canada must carry a passport from their native country and may also need a visa. For further information contact the Bahamian Ministry of Foreign Affairs (☎ 323-5578) in Nassau or the Bahamian Consulate in your home country. A comprehensive list of entry requirements is available on the tourist board's website at www.bahamas.com by clicking on the Travel Info button.

A Bahamas flag waves in the breeze.

Time

The Bahamas is on Eastern Standard Time (EST), the same as Miami and New York, and five hours behind GMT. When it's noon in The Bahamas, it's 5pm in London, 9am in San Francisco and 2am the following day in Syndey. Daylight saving time (EDT) is observed from the last Sunday in April through the last Sunday in October.

Money

The Bahamian dollar is tied directly to the U.S. dollar—that is, US$1=$1Bah. U.S. currency is readily accepted throughout The Bahamas. Major credit cards and traveler's checks are accepted at all major resorts. At smaller resorts you should check in advance. Even in Nassau and Freeport, many smaller establishments—restaurants, stores, etc.—do not accept credit cards. In the Out Islands be prepared to pay cash for transactions, though many of the larger and more established resorts will accept credit cards (usually MasterCard, Visa and American Express). There are ATMs in Nassau and Freeport, but don't expect to find them easily in the Out Islands.

Electricity

Electrical current throughout the islands runs at 110 volts/60 cycles, the same as the U.S. and Canada. Plugs are all U.S.-standard with two flat prongs (often polarized), and many establishments have grounded three-prong (two flat, one round) plugs. Adapters are available in hardware stores. Electrical service is generally quite dependable, even on the more remote islands.

Weights & Measures

The Bahamas uses the imperial system. Speed-limit signs appear in miles per hour, temperature in degrees Fahrenheit, weight in ounces and pounds, length in inches and feet, and volume in pints, quarts and gallons. Measurements in this book are given in both imperial and metric units, except for specific references within dive site descriptions, which are given in imperial units only. For reference, use the conversion chart inside the back cover of this book.

What to Bring

Dress tends to be casual throughout the islands. A supply of shorts, short-sleeve shirts and tennis shoes will suffice for most occasions. In Nassau and Freeport, women may want to bring a light dress for casinos, nightclubs and more elegant restaurants. Men will want slacks and a casual dress shirt for the same places. A light rain jacket can come in handy. During the winter months a light sweater or jacket is advised for the evenings. Please refrain from wearing beachwear in town in Freeport or Nassau, though attitudes are a little more relaxed in the Out Islands.

For diving, a diveskin or thin wetsuit provides protection from stings and abrasions in the summer months. In the winter you will want to wear at least a 3mm wetsuit. High-quality rental gear and some repair facilities are available nearly everywhere if you should experience problems with your own gear. Almost all dive operations allow and encourage computer diving.

Underwater Photography

Major dive resorts such as Stuart Cove's Dive Bahamas (New Providence) or UNEXSO (Grand Bahama) have excellent dedicated photo operations featuring daily print and E6 slide processing, equipment rental and instruction.

Shark Photography

Photographing sharks may be one of the greatest challenges in open-ocean underwater photography. With other large-predator wildlife photography, the photographer wields a telephoto lens from a relatively safe distance. In shark photography, however, your first goal is to get as close to your subject as possible.

Technical excellence and safety are your main considerations. The best way to stay safe is to be knowledgeable about your subjects. Be sure to listen to your divemasters—they know the individual sharks in their area. In terms of attitude, sharks differ by species. There are over 300 species of sharks, but only a handful are considered man-eaters or, more precisely, man-biters. Photographing a mako, tiger, oceanic whitetip, great hammerhead, great white or other aggressive blue-water shark requires a different approach than a Caribbean reef or nurse shark.

Any shark can be unpredictable. Watch for signs of aggressive behavior, such as the lowering of pectoral fins, arching of the back or a sideways swiping of the head. When this occurs, be prepared to retreat for a moment. Some situations demand a shark suit or shark cage, while others allow for less-elaborate precautions. You should wear a dark wetsuit and black gloves on shark feeds—bright colors are attractive, and pale hands can be mistaken for food.

To achieve professional images, use the shortest focal length lens with which you are comfortable. A Nikonos with a 24mm, 20mm or 15mm lens is good for fast-action situations. In more stable situations, a housed system with a 20mm lens is good for full-body shots, while a 24mm or 35mm lens works for close-ups. A 20 to 35mm zoom lens is the ideal tool. If you're nervy enough to get within 2 to 3ft (.6 to .9m) of your subject, a full-frame fisheye lens (14 to 16mm) is an excellent tool.

For lighting, strobes are essential but present special considerations. Sharks are dark on top and light on the bottom, so it is easy to overexpose the belly—be sure to consider this in your strobe-to-subject distance and strobe power. A single strobe works, but two are preferable. Power down the strobe aimed at the belly—use it to soften and feather hard shadows. Your primary strobe will illuminate the subject's face and back, as well as the mask of any diver in the frame. Expect the sharks to muddy the water. To minimize backscatter, use oblique angles and avoid lighting the water between you and the subject.

Outside these major centers, access to photographic equipment and supplies is limited. It's wise to bring all the film and batteries you think you may need, plus some extra. Repair facilities are limited, so you may want to bring backup bodies and lenses.

Business Hours

Business hours vary but usually run from 9am to 5 or 6pm Monday through Saturday. Few stores open on Sunday. Banking hours are from 9:30am to 3pm Monday through Thursday and 9:30am to 5pm on Friday.

Accommodations

The style of accommodations available depends largely on your island of choice. In the Nassau area (which includes Cable Beach and Paradise Island), there are no fewer than 65 guest houses, villas, self-catering apartments, small resorts and hotels. Lodgings range in size from four-room bed-and-breakfasts to elaborate resorts with thousands of rooms. The Out Islands deliver a more low-key and relaxed vacation experience. Hotels tend to be smaller and more casual, though some establishments offer very attractive, subdued island elegance. There are even a couple of Club Meds with dedicated dive operations for those who prefer an active, structured experience.

Divers should look into the dive packages—which include airfare, diving, accommodations and sometimes food—offered by most professional dive operators. It's often easier and less expensive than booking each element of your trip separately. Keep in mind that these packages are designed primarily for people who want to dive every day. If you're looking for a more varied vacation, explore other options to find what is right for you.

Prices during the low season (April through September) are often significantly lower than in the winter high season (October through March). A complete list of accommodations is available from the tourist board.

A small cottage on Walker's Cay offers tropical elegance.

Dining & Food

As you might expect, much Bahamian cuisine revolves around the bounty of the ocean. Fresh seafood, such as grouper, dolphinfish (mahimahi), snapper, wahoo, shrimp, lobster and conch, is found on every menu. The islands' proximity to the U.S. also allows for a dependable supply of good-quality meats. Local specialties include side dishes like peas and rice (a rich, lightly spiced blend of rice and pigeon peas), johnnycake or some of the best macaroni and cheese anywhere (thick, crusty, rich and bubbling around the edges). Check out the national dessert, guava duff, and be sure to visit some of the open-air conch stands for fresh, delectable conch salad, usually served up with some juicy local gossip (*sip-sip* in the local lingo). In Nassau and Freeport you'll find a more international and cosmopolitan array of restaurants and dishes than in the Out Islands, which feature more casual island establishments.

Conch Salad

Conch is ubiquitous throughout The Bahamas. The queen conch (*Strombus gigas*) is one of the largest snails in the sea. It feeds in sand flats, of which there are plenty in The Bahamas. Conch salad, conch fritters, stewed conch, conch souse, cracked conch, scorched conch—the ways in which it is prepared are numerous, and each is an island delicacy. Of all the recipes, conch salad is the most popular.

Conch salad recipes are as varied as the islands of The Bahamas. Some people use a bird pepper (a small and very spicy red pepper that will burn the hair off your nostrils), splitting it in half and rubbing the conch before dicing. In the Abacos, conch salad is often served swimming in sweet-and-sour orange juice. The following is a good basic recipe:

   1 large or 2 small conchs
   1 small tomato
   ¼ green pepper
   ½ medium yellow onion
   1 Scotch bonnet (habanero) chile pepper
   salt
   lime or sour orange
   sweet orange (optional)

Rinse conch and score horizontally and vertically halfway through the flesh about ¼-inch apart. Cut into ¼-inch squares. Dice the tomato, mince the onion and the green pepper, and mix with conch. Salt to taste, about ¼- to ½-teaspoon. Add chile pepper to taste—be cautious! Squeeze juice of one lime or one sour orange over ingredients. Add juice of sweet orange if desired. Enjoy!

Shopping

As the Bahamas has no import tax on luxury goods meant for resale, the larger shopping areas such Nassau's Bay Street or the Freeport/Port Lucaya area offer excellent duty-free shopping. Savings can be very good, but the wise shopper should be aware of what they would pay for similar items back home. Duty-free does not always translate to less expensive. The best bargains are found on perfume, jewelry and gems, watches and clocks, photographic equipment, leather goods, and fine china and glassware. You'll find many internationally known and respected brand names and shops represented here.

U.S. citizens are allowed to bring back up to US$600 in duty-free goods. One liter of duty-free alcohol (wine, liqueur or liquor) and five cartons of cigarettes per legal-age individual are allowed. Gifts of up US$50 in value may be sent home duty-free.

For local items, look to straw markets—markets devoted mainly to straw goods such as belts, hats and bags—in the larger communities, as well as in the Out Islands. Local arts and crafts made of wood, straw and shell, as well as clothing, are readily available. Shopping bags, hats, belts, place mats and other items make nice souvenirs, but be sure they are actually island-made, as many items are imported. Bargaining is rare in the shops but is expected in the open-air markets.

Shopping for fruits and vegetables at a local open-air market.

Activities & Attractions

The Bahamas has long been recognized as a mecca for vacationers seeking to indulge themselves in the sea, the sun, the sand and the simple pleasures of life. If your tastes run to shopping, elaborate beach sports, golf, gambling, dining and nightlife, you'll want to stick to the Nassau area of New Providence and the Freeport/Port Lucaya area of Grand Bahama.

Don't expect such a wide array of activities in the Out Islands, where relaxation will be your primary activity. One worthwhile diversion is a road trip. You can see ruins of Loyalist plantations, sites of natural interest, limestone formations, caves and many inviting isolated beaches. An excellent source for detailed activities and attractions information throughout the islands is Lonely Planet's *Bahamas, Turks & Caicos*.

Nature Preserves

The Bahamas boasts many nature preserves worthy of a visit. A complete list of nature preserves is available from the **Bahamas National Trust** (☎ 393-1317) in Nassau. A visit to the property, which has a collection of orchids and other wildflowers and offers excellent bird-watching, is a rewarding trip in itself. Other standouts on New Providence include Nassau's **Botanical Gardens**, which features 600-plus species of tropical plants spread across 26 acres (11 hectares). Also in Nassau, the **Ardastra Gardens & Zoo** boasts an extensive collection of both indigenous and nonnative animals— the West Indian flamingos are a popular highlight.

A visit to the **Garden of the Grove** on Grand Bahama is essential. This 11-acre (4.5-hectare) garden offers a fern gully, four small waterfalls and a collection of more than 5,000 species of exotic plants and shrubs from around the world. Another must-see is **Lucayan National Park**, which offers an excellent view of the true Bahamian natural world. It includes a limestone plateau riddled

Nassau's resident flamingos.

25

with caves opening into a massive underwater system, as well as several distinct shoreline and inland ecosystems.

The Out Islands have fewer maintained parks but do have areas set aside for protection by the Bahamas National Trust. Bird-watching is excellent throughout the islands. Uninhabited locales such as Conception Island are nesting sites for shore- and waterbirds and resting spots for migrating birds. Several beaches are nesting grounds for green turtles. Allan's Cay, in the Northern Exumas, is home to the largest breeding population of the Allan's Cay iguana. Other endemic sub-species of iguanas are found on San Salvador, Mayaguana, Andros and several of the other Exuma Cays.

Kayaking or canoeing among the mangroves is an excellent way to explore the natural world of The Bahamas. These small, quiet, unobtrusive craft provide a perfect platform for bird-watching and photography in these animal-rich environments. Also consider packing a mask, snorkel and fins—the mangroves are a nursery for numerous juvenile fish and invertebrate species. Take time to peek among the roots and you may be surprised at what you find.

Historical Sites

Historical sites are a draw in several of the Out Islands. Visit the ruins of **Watling's Castle** overlooking French Bay on the south end of San Salvador. From 1860 to 1926, San Salvador was known as Watling's Island, after Captain John Watling, a pirate turned cotton-plantation owner. These are the remains of his estate.

San Salvador's Watling's Castle.

On Cat Island, **Mount Alvernia Hermitage** sits on The Bahamas's highest point—a towering 206ft (79m) above sea level. The hermitage was the home of Father Jerome, an Anglican minister who lived the life of an ascetic while building churches and doing good deeds for local residents. He lived in the hermitage from 1939 until his death in 1956.

Natural sites of historical significance, including Columbus' landing sites and caves in which native Lucayans hid from raiding Caribs, are also numerous. Be certain to visit some of the many small settlements and pass some time in a small pub speaking with the local folks. It's a great way to get tips about little-known spots and collect some local lore.

Sailing & Regattas

With its multiple ports, short crossings and generally favorable weather, The Bahamas is a prized cruising ground for sailors. Chartered sailboats, either bareboat or with captain and crew, are readily available. Perhaps the greatest concentration of sailboats is that found in Elizabeth Harbour at Great Exuma in autumn, when literally hundreds of vessels gather.

Favored cruising areas are the Exuma Cays, with many protected anchorages, and the waters around the Abaco chain. The most important feature of both areas is that you are always within sight of land. Marsh Harbour on Great Abaco is an excellent outfitting spot from which to depart for the northern cays. Green Turtle Cay and the other Loyalist Cays offer a bizarre, quaint atmosphere that evokes New England, but with a distinct tropical flair.

The primary dangers to sailors are the abundance of shallow reefs and the ever-changing nature of the shallows and sandbars. The shallows can change with each storm and demand a sharp, experienced eye and up-to-date charts. For those who are inexperienced but want to get out on the water in a casual fashion, try renting a small Hobie Cat or a Sunfish.

Also worthy of attention are the traditional Bahamian sloop regattas. These races are limited to locally made Bahamian sailing sloops. These single-masted vessels were historically called smack fishing boats. Participating boats are made with painstaking attention to traditional construction details. The largest competition is the Family Island Regatta, held annually out of George Town on Great Exuma. This is strictly a local affair. Non-Bahamians who wish to participate as crew must get permission from the ruling committees.

Bahamian smack fishing boats are made with strict attention to traditional details.

Fishing

The fishing potential of The Bahamas consistently gets rave reviews from sport-fishing enthusiasts around the world. Deep-sea fishing for a broad variety of blue-water fish is one focus, while a second major draw is the world-class bonefishing. Top fishing destinations include Walker's Cay (north end of the Abacos), Bimini and the Bimini chain and San Salvador, as well as New Providence and Grand Bahama.

In reality, the entire country is rich with game fish. The "top" destinations are simply the most convenient and have good marina support. What you're fishing for varies with the season, but includes amberjacks, barracuda, blackfin tuna, blue marlins, bluefin tuna, dolphinfish, groupers, kingfish, sailfish, tarpon, wahoos and white marlins. In fact, Ernest Hemingway was the first person known to have boated an intact giant bluefin tuna, a feat he accomplished in the waters around Bimini during the bluefin's annual migration. Bimini also boasts the largest fish caught to date in The Bahamas—a monster 1,060lb (481kg) blue marlin.

Bonefishing is excellent around any island that features shallow flats. Bimini, Cat Island, Eleuthera, the Abacos, the Exumas and Andros have great reputations.

There are plenty of sportfishing tournaments every year—some are for fun, others for big money prizes. The Exumas host two bonefishing tournaments— one on Staniel Cay in August and the other on Great Exuma in October. Nearly all tournaments promote a catch-and-release policy.

Sportfishing charters are readily available at major marinas. If you ask around on any of the Out Islands, it's usually easy to find a knowledgeable local bone-fishing guide.

Golf

New Providence has two championship golf courses. In Cable Beach you'll find the Arnold Palmer–designed **Radisson Cable Beach Golf Course**, a challenging 18-hole course dotted with plenty of water and sand traps. The second is found on the south-west corner of the island, on the grounds of the Clarion South Ocean Resort. The **Clarion Resort South Ocean Golf Course** is an 18-hole PGA Championship–rated course designed by Joe Lee. It is considered the most challenging on the island.

Grand Bahama features several championship courses. The Princess Resort of-fers visitors the **Emerald & Ruby Golf Courses**. These twin 18-hole USGA-rated courses are par-72 Dick Wilson creations. The **Fortune Hills Golf & Country Club** is a nine-hole course also designed by Dick Wilson. The 18-hole course at the **Lucaya Golf & Country Club** is considered sedate but remains highly rated.

Casinos

While you're on New Providence, a visit to Paradise Island's **Atlantis** is a must. This very elaborate resort complex is one of the largest in the world. From a dis-tance, it's monolithic. Up close you can appreciate the marine theme—the external structure is decorated with massive sculptures of seahorses, seashells such as Triton's trumpets and nautiluses, various billfish and more. The complex features eight different marine environments, including the world's largest fish tank, which boasts a clear Plexiglas walk-through tunnel replete with sharks, turtles and rays. The casino, developed by Sun International of South African Sun City fame, is the largest in the greater Caribbean region, featuring 78 gaming tables and 980 slot machines. At the Nassau Marriott in Cable Beach, the huge **Crystal Palace Casino** features more than 800 slots and more than 70 gaming tables. Both Nassau casinos have nightly floor shows.

In Freeport you'll find the **Bahamas Princess Casino** at the Bahamas Princess Country Club. It features more than 400 slot machines, more than 60 gaming tables and offshore betting on major sporting events. Another casino on Grand Bahama is at the newly refurbished and expanded **Lucayan Beach & Golf Resort**.

Junkanoo

Of all Bahamian celebrations, none reflects the heart of Bahamian culture more than Junkanoo. Though reminiscent of New Orleans' Mardi Gras or the down-island Caribbean carnivals, Junkanoo is nonetheless wholeheartedly and unabashedly Bahamian. The celebration dates from the 18th century, when slaves were given three days respite at Christmastime. Initially, it was a celebration derivative of West African traditions, but over the centuries it has absorbed other cultures and is now a thoroughly Bahamian occasion.

The action begins as early as 3am on Boxing Day, December 26. The start of Junkanoo is heralded by the pounding of goatskin drums, the blaring of horns and the blowing of whistles. The relentless *ka-LIK, ka-LIK, ka-LIK* of the parade's cowbells sets the pulse and urges the people forward. Elaborate costumes are the official dress of the day—costumes that have been lovingly crafted and often kept absolutely secret until their unveiling. Groups called "shacks" get together to build their costumes around themes, competing for the honor of best costumes, best performance and best music. The dancing, drinking and tireless partying runs throughout the day. A second Junkanoo takes place on New Year's Day. Some islands have a third major Junkanoo celebration on June 10th, Bahamian Independence Day.

The largest Junkanoo is in Nassau, but each island has its own unique celebration. Standard characters include the Bunce—locals pronounce it "Boonce"—a forest-dwelling gremlin covered in a sheet who is carried around to scare and joke with local children. Bunce is a true piece of Bahamian folklore, and some locals still take measures to protect themselves from this night-roaming demon. During the Junkanoo ceremonies the Bunce is captured and buried.

The music of Junkanoo, called Goombay, is an infectious, upbeat, repetitive, highly rhythmic and hypnotic stream of sound. Add together the clicking of sticks, the rattle of maracas and the low moaning of conch-shell horns and you've got the sounds of a Goombay band. The terms Junkanoo and Goombay are often used interchangeably, and they boil down to the same thing—a great excuse for a "big fun" party. To learn a bit more about the celebrations, try stopping by Nassau's Junkanoo Expo in the old wharfside customs building off Bay Street.

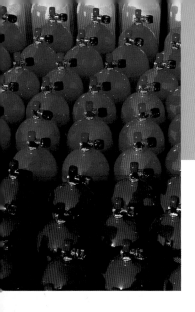

Diving Health & Safety

The Bahamas is a generally healthy destination and poses few particular health concerns for most visitors. Inoculations are not required unless you are arriving from a high-risk country, and this would be for the protection of other visitors and residents.

The biggest concern visitors will encounter is the sun. Be certain to pack a high-quality sunscreen with a high SPF (sun protection factor) and wear a hat or cover-up when possible. Carry pure aloe vera gel in case you do get burned—a liberal application (as much as your skin will absorb) will help prevent blistering and peeling. You may also want to carry a topical antihistamine for relief of any minor irritating stings from marine creatures. Also be sure to drink plenty of water to prevent dehydration.

The U.S. Centers for Disease Control & Prevention regularly posts updates on health-related concerns around the world specifically for travelers. Contact the CDC by fax or visit their website. Call (toll-free from the U.S.) ☎ 888-232-3299 and request Document 000005 to receive a list of documents available by fax. The website is www.cdc.gov.

Pre-Trip Preparation

Your general state of health, diving skill level and specific equipment needs are the three most important factors that impact any dive trip. If you honestly assess these before you leave, you'll be well on your way to assuring a safe dive trip.

First, if you're not in shape, start exercising. Second, if you haven't dived for a while (six months is too long) and your skills are rusty, do a local dive with an experienced buddy or take a scuba review course. Finally, inspect your dive gear. Feeling good physically, diving with experience and with reliable equipment will not only increase your safety, but will also enhance your enjoyment underwater.

At least a month before your trip, inspect your dive gear. Remember, your regulator should be serviced annually, whether you've used it or not. If you use a dive computer and can replace the battery yourself, change it before the trip or buy a

Diving & Flying

Most divers in The Bahamas arrive by plane. While it's fine to dive soon *after* flying, it's important to remember that your last dive should be completed at least 12 hours (some experts advise 24 hours, particularly after repetitive dives) *before* your flight to minimize the risk of decompression sickness, caused by residual nitrogen in the blood.

spare to take along. Otherwise, send the computer to the manufacturer for a battery replacement.

If possible, find out if the dive center rents or services the type of gear you own. If not, you might want to take spare parts or even spare gear. A spare mask is always a good idea.

Purchase any additional equipment you might need, such as a dive light and tank marker light for night diving, a line reel for wreck diving, etc. Make sure you have at least a whistle attached to your BC. Better yet, add a marker tube (also known as a safety sausage or come-to-me).

About a week before taking off, do a final check of your gear, grease o-rings, check batteries and assem-

Quality training by knowledgeable instructors is a central element of The Bahamas' dive industry.

ble a save-a-dive kit. This kit should at minimum contain extra mask and fin straps, snorkel keeper, mouthpiece, valve cap, zip ties and o-rings. Don't forget to pack a first-aid kit and medications such as decongestants, ear drops, antihistamines and seasickness tablets. Be sure to bring a sufficient amount of any personal medication.

Tips for Evaluating a Dive Boat

Dive boats can be anything from fragile skiffs to elegant live-aboards. Before departure, take a good look at the craft you will be diving from. A well-outfitted dive boat has communication with on-shore services. It also carries oxygen, a recall device and a first-aid kit. A well-prepared crew will give a thorough pre-dive briefing that explains procedures for dealing with an emergency when divers are in the water. The briefing also explains how divers should enter the water and get back onboard. A larger boat should have a shaded area and a supply of fresh drinking water.

If there is a strong current, the crew might provide a special descent line and should be able to throw out a drift line from the stern. For deep dives, the crew should hang a safety tank at 15ft (5m). On night dives, a good boat will have powerful lights, including a strobe light.

When carrying groups, a good crew will get everyone's name on the dive roster and do a verbal check to verify that every diver has returned to the vessel before departure, so they can initiate an immediate search if a diver is missing. This is something you should always verify.

A sailboat plies the waters off Eleuthera.

Signaling Devices

Occasionally a diver becomes lost or is left behind at a dive site—make sure this never happens to you! A diver is extremely difficult to locate in the water, so always dive with a signaling device of some sort, preferably more than one.

One of the best signaling devices and the easiest to carry is a whistle. Even the little ones are extremely effective. Use a zip tie to attach one permanently to your BC. Even better, though more expensive, is a loud bullhorn that connects to the inflator hose. You simply push a button to let out a blast. It does require air from your tank to function, though.

In order to be seen as well as heard, you should also carry a marker tube (also called a safety sausage or come-to-me). The best ones are bright in color and about 10ft (3m) high. They roll up and can easily fit into a BC pocket or be clipped onto a D-ring. They're inflated orally or with a regulator. Some allow you to insert a dive light into the tube—a nice feature when it's dark.

Other signaling aides include mirrors, flares and dye markers, but these have limited reliability. A simple dive light is particularly versatile. Not only can it be used during the day for looking into crevices and crannies, it also comes in handy for nighttime signaling. Some even have a special strobe feature. When you're diving during the day, consider carrying at least a small light—you might encounter an unexpected night dive and be happy to have it.

Medical & Recompression Facilities

The Bahamas has a network of government-administrated clinics that offer general medical care in settlements throughout the Out Islands as well as private clinics in major towns. For serious medical problems you will need to be transported to Nassau or Freeport. The following is a list of the major hospitals and clinics:

Nassau

Doctor's Hospital
☎ 322-8411

Lyford Cay Hospital
☎ 362-4025

Princess Margaret Hospital
☎ 322-2861

Freeport

Rand Memorial Hospital
☎ 352-6735

Lucayan Medical Centre
☎ 352-7288

Sunrise Medical Centre
☎ 373-3333

The Bahamas' sole professional hyperbaric chamber is open seven days a week and is well staffed with highly skilled personnel. Consult your dive operator for emergency procedures and always call DAN first in the event of a dive emergency:

Bahamas Hyperbaric Centre
Lyford Cay, Cable Beach, New Providence
☎ 362-5765

DAN

Divers Alert Network (DAN) is an international membership association of individuals and organizations sharing a common interest in diving and safety. It operates a 24-hour diving emergency hotline in the U.S.: ☎ **919-684-8111 or 919-684-4DAN** (-4326). The latter accepts collect calls in a dive emergency. Though DAN does not directly provide medical care, it does provide advice on early treatment, evacuation and hyperbaric treatment of diving-related injuries. Divers should contact DAN for assistance as soon as a diving emergency is suspected.

DAN membership is reasonably priced and includes DAN TravelAssist, a membership benefit that covers medical air evacuation from anywhere in the world for any illness or injury. For a small additional fee, divers can get secondary insurance coverage for decompression illness. For membership details, contact DAN at ☎ 800-446-2671 in the U.S. or ☎ 919-684-2948 elsewhere. DAN can also be reached at www.diversalertnetwork.org.

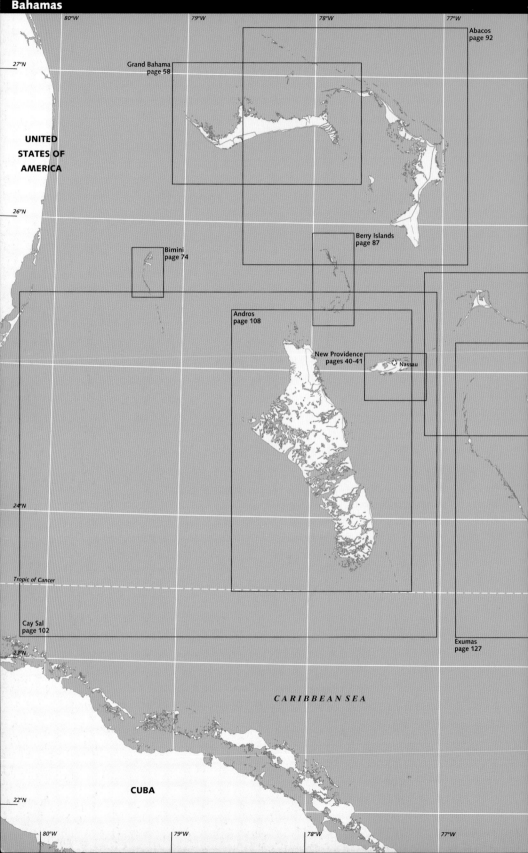

27°N
80°W   79°W   78°W   77°W

Abacos
page 92

Grand Bahama
page 58

**UNITED
STATES OF
AMERICA**

26°N

Berry Islands
page 87

Bimini
page 74

Andros
page 108

New Providence
pages 40-41

Nassau

24°N

Tropic of Cancer

Cay Sal
page 102

23°N

Exumas
page 127

CARIBBEAN SEA

CUBA

22°N

80°W   79°W   78°W   77°W

6°W   75°W   74°W   73°W   72°W

27°N

26°N

Eleuthera
page 118

ATLANTIC OCEAN

25°N

Cat Island
page 135

THE

BAHAMAS

San Salvador
page 151

24°N

Tropic of Cancer

23°N

Long Island Group
page 141

TURKS AND

CAICOS (UK)

6°W   75°W   74°W   73°W

Diving in The Bahamas

It's difficult to characterize the dive experience of The Bahamas within a few features. The variety of destinations up and down the archipelago run the gamut of diving environments at every experience level. Want to see big animals? You can dive with sharks, swim with dolphins and may encounter manta rays, whale sharks or pods of pilot whales. Prefer shallow reefs? Spend hours watching marine creatures. Fascinated by caves and caverns? Check out the famed oceanic and landlocked blue holes. Love to sail over walls or explore wrecks? Take your pick from world-class examples of both.

Water conditions are mostly optimal. The flat limestone islands represent the archetype of the traditional dive destination. The country is without a single river and the porous limestone absorbs nearly all rainfall, so there is no runoff to degrade water visibility. That said, visibility does vary with the wind direction, as is common with the juxtaposition of shallow, broad sand areas and extremely deep blue-water troughs. When the wind blows across the bank toward the edge of a deep channel, water motion stirs up the bottom and reduces visibility. Conversely, a wind that blows across the deep blue pushes crystal-clear water onto the reef and visibility improves greatly. Expect visibility to average between 80 and 120ft (24 and 37m), with peaks of 150ft (46m) or more and lows of 30ft (9.1m) and below. Current conditions vary, but are generally imperceptible to mild, with a few specific exceptions.

Dive operators throughout The Bahamas are consistently competent. The rule is full-service operations with contemporary boats, equipment sales and service, on-site compressors and well-trained staff members with a thorough knowledge of the area and a true love of what they are doing. Most truly professional dive operations are members of the Bahamas Dive Association and live up to the organization's standards. Dive operations vary primarily in the size of groups on the boats and the type of diving in which they specialize. Do your research and ask enough questions to find an operator appropriate to your own style of diving.

Snorkeling

Virtually every dive operator in The Bahamas has an active snorkeling program, often on dedicated snorkel boats. The multitude of shallow reefs makes this an ideal place for individuals who prefer to experience the ocean unencumbered by scuba gear. Some dive operators offer full-day snorkeling activities, which incorporate beach parties, fishing, nature excursions and more. If someone in your group doesn't dive, these programs may well tempt the nondiver into taking the plunge.

Though less formalized than dive training, snorkeling instruction is important for safety.

Certification & Specialty Courses

Every professional dive operation in The Bahamas is associated with one or more professional certifying agencies. These include (but are not limited to) PADI, NAUI, CMAS and BSAC. PADI is by far the dominant organization. If you're new to the sport, you can take a full Open Water certification course, which takes five days and includes at least four open water dives. Many operators also offer a simple resort course—a non-certifying course that includes two hours of pool training and an instructor-escorted dive to a shallow reef. Some operators have multilingual staff, who can offer instruction in languages other than English. If you have not been diving in a while, you may want to inquire about the possibility of doing a refresher course, either at home or upon arrival in the islands.

One option is to do your classroom and pool work at home and complete your Open Water dives in the warm waters of The Bahamas. Every dive operator in The Bahamas is a universal referral center, which means if you do your classroom work at home, you can do your open-water training dives with any Bahamian operator, no matter which certifying agency you train with.

Youngsters can qualify for PADI's Junior Certification Program, in which a responsible child as young as 10 years old can be certified to dive to 40ft (12m). Diving with a parent is permitted at ages 10 and 11. At age 12, any responsible adult may accompany the Junior Diver. When the diver turns 13, the junior certification rolls over into a full Open Water certification.

Certified divers are eligible for a wide range of advanced and specialty courses. Some dive operators offer training in nitrox diving, rebreather systems and diver propulsion vehicles (DPVs). Stuart Cove's Dive Bahamas, UNEXSO and Nassau Scuba Center offer shark-feeding courses, while UNEXSO's Dolphin Experience program teaches dolphin handling and training.

Live-Aboards

The Bahamas is served by a fleet of live-aboard dive vessels based out of the U.S. as well as The Bahamas. The vessels range from monohull sailboats and catamarans to converted oil-field crew boats to elegant vessels offering casual dive schedules.

A live-aboard dive trip is ideal for those looking to maximize their in-water time and experience dive sites beyond the reach of land-based dive operations. Itineraries include some more-popular areas, while each vessel has its own special areas of expertise. All have captains and crew who are experienced in the areas they serve. Several live-aboards have film processing and resident photo pros.

Dive Site Icons

The symbols at the beginning of each dive site description provide a quick summary of some of the following characteristics present at each site:

 Good snorkeling or free-diving site.

 Remains or partial remains of a wreck can be seen at this site.

 Sheer wall or drop-off.

 Deep dive. Features of this dive occur in water deeper than 90ft (27m).

 Strong currents may be encountered at this site.

 Strong surge (the horizontal movement of water caused by waves) may be encountered at this site.

 Drift dive. Because of strong currents and/or difficulty in anchoring, a drift dive is recommended at this site.

 Beach/shore dive. This site can be accessed from shore.

 Caves are a prominent feature of this site. Only experienced cave divers should explore inner cave areas.

 Marine preserve. Special regulations apply in this area.

Pisces Rating System for Dives & Divers

The dive sites in this book are rated according to the following diver skill-level rating system. These are not absolute ratings but apply to divers at a particular time, diving at a particular place. For instance, someone unfamiliar with prevailing conditions might be considered a novice diver at one dive area, but an intermediate diver at another, more familiar location.

Novice: A novice diver should be accompanied by an instructor, divemaster or advanced diver on all dives. A novice diver generally fits the following profile:
◆ basic scuba certification from an internationally recognized certifying agency
◆ dives infrequently (less than one trip a year)
◆ logged fewer than 25 total dives
◆ little or no experience diving in similar waters and conditions
◆ dives no deeper than 60ft (18m)

Intermediate: An intermediate diver generally fits the following profile:
◆ may have participated in some form of continuing diver education
◆ logged between 25 and 100 dives
◆ dives no deeper than 130ft (40m)
◆ has been diving in similar waters and conditions within the last six months

Advanced: An advanced diver generally fits the following profile:
◆ advanced certification
◆ has been diving for more than two years and logged over 100 dives
◆ has been diving in similar waters and conditions within the last six months

Regardless of your skill level, you should be in good physical condition and know your limitations. If you are uncertain of your own level of expertise for a particular site, ask the advice of a local dive instructor. He or she is best qualified to assess your abilities based on the site's prevailing dive conditions. Ultimately, however, you must decide if you are capable of making a particular dive, a decision that should take into account your level of training, recent experience and physical condition, as well as the conditions at the site. Remember that conditions can change at any time, even during a dive.

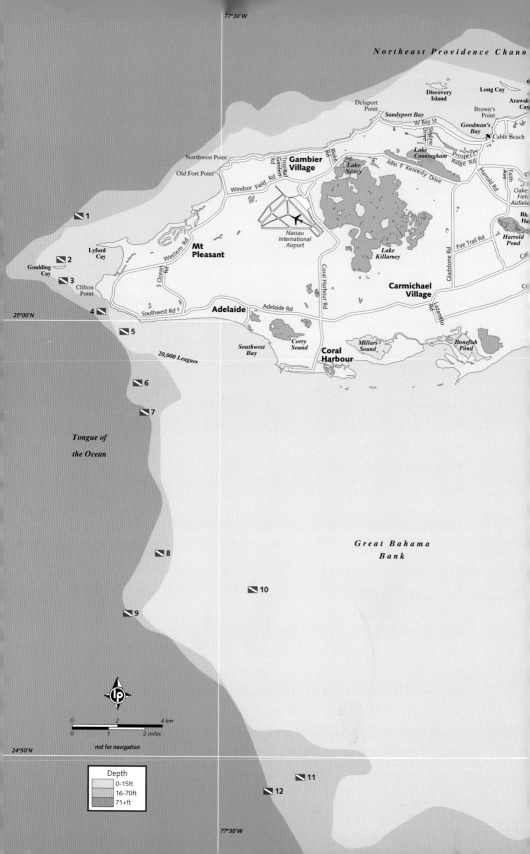

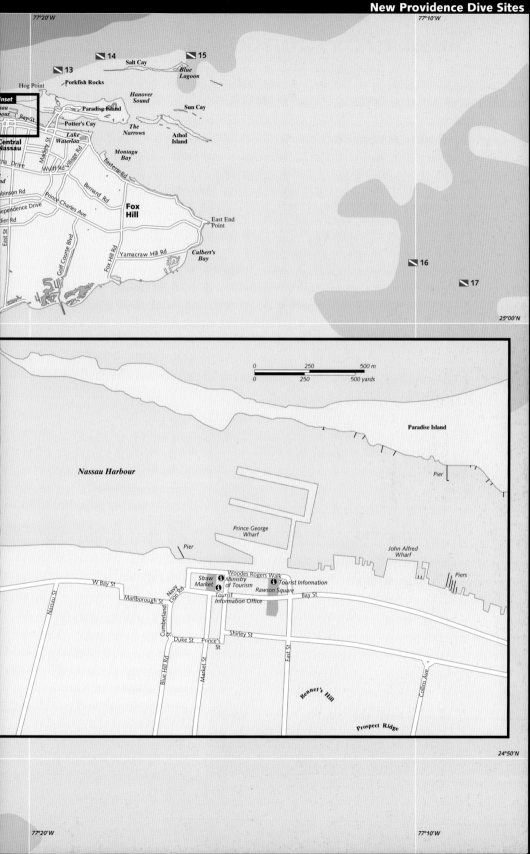

77°20'W

77°10'W

14   Salt Cay

13   Porkfish Rocks

15   Blue Lagoon

Hog Point

Inset

sau
our

Bay St.

Hanover
Sound

Paradise Island

Sun Cay

Potter's Cay

Central
Nassau

Lake
Waterloo

The
Narrows

Athol
Island

Drive

Montagu
Bay

Robinson Rd

Bernard Rd

Fox
Hill

Independence Drive

Prince Charles Ave

East End
Point

dier Rd

East St

Golf Course Blvd

Fox Hill Rd

Yamacraw Hill Rd

Culbert's
Bay

16

17

25°00'N

Paradise Island

Nassau Harbour

Pier

0   250   500 m
0   250   500 yards

Prince George
Wharf

John Alfred
Wharf

Pier

Piers

W Bay St

Marlborough St

Nassau St

Navy Lion Rd

Straw
Market

Woodes Rogers Walk
Ministry
of Tourism

Tourist Information

Rawson Square

Bay St

Cumberland St

Tourist
Information Office

Blue Hill Rd

Duke St   Prince's
St

Market St

Shirley St

East St

Collins Ave

Bennet's Hill

Prospect Ridge

24°50'N

77°20'W

77°10'W

New Providence Dive Sites

Divers in New Providence benefit from the excellent tourism infrastructure and well-developed dive industry of Nassau and nearby Paradise Island, as well as from the island's rich and varied marine environment.

New Providence sits right above the Great Bahamas Canyon, a deep oceanic trench with walls that rise 14,060ft (4,285m) from the canyon bottom to the surrounding seabed. Its three main branches—the Tongue of the Ocean, the Northwest Providence Channel and the Northeast Providence Channel—converge directly north of New Providence. Due to this geographic positioning, walls wrap around the island's west edge and across its northwest coast. The Tongue of the Ocean, dropping south 120 miles (193km) directly into the heart of the Great Bahama Bank, offers mile after mile of incredible walls and is a perfect conduit for cruising pelagics.

In addition to the notable walls, New Providence boasts plenty of expansive shallow coral gardens. A combination of shoals, reefs and barrier islands stretches clear across the north side of the Great Bahama Bank to western Eleuthera. The reefs north of New Providence are spur-and-groove formations. To the south, sand flats strewn with coral heads stretch down past the Exumas and beyond.

Nassau's two main claims to fame, however, are wrecks and sharks. On the southwest corner, Wreck City is a playground of wrecks of many different types, most sunk on purpose both for divers and for the film industry. One of Nassau's most important attractions is its shark diving. Caribbean reef sharks, along with nurse sharks and occasional other visitors, gather in groups of three dozen and more to feed, intimidating and entertaining visiting divers in the process.

Shark dives are a primary attraction off New Providence.

New Providence Dive Sites

	Good Snorkeling	Novice	Intermediate	Advanced
1 Tunnel Wall			●	
2 Goulding Cay	●	●		
3 Willaurie			●	
4 The Bond Wrecks		●		
5 Cessna Wreck (Cessna Wall)			●	
6 Caribe Breeze	●		●	
7 Runway, Bahama Mama & Shark Bowl			●	
8 Pumpkin Patch & Karen's Reef			●	
9 Razorback & Playpen			●	
10 Southwest Reef	●	●		
11 Shark Wall, Shark Arena & Edward Williams			●	
12 Hole in the Head			●	
13 The Graveyard (The Shipyard)			●	
14 De La Salle			●	
15 Fish Hotel	●	●		
16 Barracuda Shoals			●	
17 Lost Ocean Blue Hole	●	●		

1 Tunnel Wall

In unfavorable weather Tunnel Wall makes a satisfactory alternative to the more-exposed southwest sites. The limestone bottom supports plenty of soft corals and low-lying hard corals, and you'll find much larger coral structures over the edge of the wall. The wall begins at 30ft and gradually slopes to 80 to 100ft before taking a more severe angle down. There are many small tunnels and arches, as well as a larger cavern at about 70ft.

Location: North of Lyford Cay

Depth Range: 30-130ft+ (9.1-40m+)

Access: Boat

Expertise Rating: Intermediate

Lampton's Wall, an adjacent site to the west, features similar contours. To the east, just north of Love Beach and the Traveler's Rest restaurant, lies **Traveler's Wall**, which also has similar features but starts about 10ft deeper. The spur-and-groove formations are more pronounced at Traveler's Wall.

2 Goulding Cay

The reef in the protected area north of Goulding Cay is a favored area for underwater movie scenes. It is also excellent for snorkeling, fish-watching and photography. Snorkelers will find the site varied and easy to approach. Though some of the areas are a bit too deep for casual snorkelers to get a close look, the elkhorn corals in the shallows reach nearly to the surface and attract lots of fish. The site is fairly well protected in most weather conditions. A number of sand bowls surrounded by corals provide good relief.

Farther offshore and east of Goulding Cay lies **Goulding Cay Wall**. This wall features black coral trees and schooling pelagics. Too far apart to swim, these two sites are done as separate dives.

Location: North of Goulding Cay

Depth Range: 10-30ft (3-9.1m)

Access: Boat

Expertise Rating: Novice

A diver confers with a curious gray angelfish.

3 *Willaurie*

After she first sank in Nassau's harbor in 1988, the *Willaurie* was refloated but again went down in a storm while under tow. The ship found her current home after she was raised once again and towed out to her present position to slip beneath the waves for the final time. A steel framework, formerly a topside

Location: South of Clifton Pier

Depth Range: 45-70ft (14-21m)

Access: Boat

Expertise Rating: Intermediate

cargo hold, crowns the vessel. The propeller is intact and glows with red encrusting sponges.

The *Willaurie* is a must-dive site. She offers everything a good wreck site should. She sits upright in clear water with a healthy coating of algaes, sponges and other invertebrates. Yellow cup corals blend with red encrusting sponges to present a brilliant tapestry.

The wreck also hosts a variety of resident marine life, including angelfish, wrasses, grunts, filefish and groupers. A huge turtle frequents the bow of the ship, which is accessed through the open cargo hold. At night the ship really comes to life. The resident turtle is often seen, as are lobsters and crabs.

The colorfully encrusted propeller of the *Willaurie*.

4 The Bond Wrecks

This site, which features two wrecks, earned its name from the wrecks' roles in James Bond "007" films. The *Tears of Allah* is an 80ft tug that was featured in the movie *Never Say Never Again*. The vessel sits upright on a sand bottom in 50ft. She is slowly developing a fuzzy sweater of hydroids and algae, upon which fish, crabs and shrimp feed.

Nearby you'll find the framework of the *Vulcan Bomber*, a mock fighter used in the filming of *Thunderball*. The skin of the mock-up has disintegrated, leaving only the ribs—it now looks like an underwater jungle gym. The wreck is

Location: South of Clifton Point

Depth Range: 30-45ft (9.1-14m)

Access: Boat

Expertise Rating: Novice

liberally draped with gorgonians, deep-water sea fans and sponges and has a rich resident fish and invertebrate population. The *Vulcan Bomber* is easily one of the most photogenic sites off New Providence.

Wreck City, New Providence

While wrecks span the entire length of The Bahamas, nowhere will you find more intact wrecks than at Wreck City on New Providence's southwest corner. These vessels were not the victims of storms or other at-sea disasters—they are part of the largest artificial reef program in The Bahamas. A dozen extraordinary wrecks of a variety of types sit on the ocean floor in this area.

A number of wrecks were placed here by the movie industry. Several factors—favorable weather and water conditions, the area's proximity to the United States and the presence of dependable, experienced surface and dive-support crews—have conspired to transform New Providence into Hollywood's underwater studio. Films with wreck scenes, including *Thunderball* and *Never Say Never Again*, have added to Wreck City's underwater topography and topside reputation.

Other Wreck City vessels were donated by outside sources or were acquired by local dive operators. Local dive operators have also been responsible for cleaning the wrecks, preparing their hulls with diver safety in mind and for their final placement.

The result of these efforts is a stimulating combination of dive profiles. Wrecked vessels include a small plane, fishing vessels, sailing craft, a mock-up of a WWII bomber, retired Bahamian Defense Force cutters and interisland freighters. Wreck depths range from 40 to 90ft (12 to 27m). The current collection is only the beginning. Plans are in place to acquire and sink several more ships, expanding the area's already-rich roster.

5 Cessna Wreck (Cessna Wall)

Near the edge of the wall, this small Cessna bit the dust in service to the movie industry for the film *Jaws IV*. Though the wreck itself is inconsequential, it serves as a central landmark for diving the wall and the shallower surrounding reef.

The plane sits at about 80ft and is surrounded by high-profile coral heads. Spend time deep on the wall before ascending to the shallower reef area. The site's proximity to the wall means that

Location: Southeast of Clifton Point

Depth Range: 50-130ft+ (15-40m+)

Access: Boat

Expertise Rating: Intermediate

the possibility of sighting pelagics is ever-present.

6   *Caribe Breeze*

Location: .5 mile (.8km) south of Southwest Bay

Depth Range: 15-70ft (4.6-21m)

Access: Boat

Expertise Rating: Intermediate

As part of the development of Wreck City, longtime New Providence dive operator Stuart Cove has been busy seeking out and placing new wrecks. On June 23, 2000, the *Caribe Breeze*, a decommissioned 200ft oil tanker, was placed a half-mile off New Providence's southwest shore. She sits upright in 70ft with her superstructure reaching to within 15ft of the surface. Her separate cargo holds are accessible, and a plan is afoot to run ropes through the interior.

The wreck's shallow depths allow her multiple purposes. Once the lines are set, she'll make a perfect training ground for wreck penetration and semi-technical sport diving. Also, she's shallow enough that snorkelers can get a glimpse of an intact wreck. The *Caribe Breeze* is destined to become a classic Bahamian wreck site.

Other Wreck City vessels include the *Anne*, which lies upside-down in 130ft to the southwest, and the *Abilin*, sitting upright in 70ft near Tunnel Wall on the north side. As with other dive sites on the northwest corner, the *Abilin* presents an ideal alternative during periods of inclement weather when the winds are coming out of the southeast.

These wrecks are relatively far apart, so they must be dived separately.

The *Caribe Breeze* above water, awaiting her final resting spot.

7 Runway, *Bahama Mama* & Shark Bowl

These three sites sit close together but are usually done as separate dives. The 110ft *Bahama Mama* served as a party boat, running booze cruises around the island before it was scuttled on the sand flat on top of the wall in 1995. Running north and east of the *Bahama Mama*, you'll see a fine strip reef with lots of snappers, grunts, groupers and smaller invertebrates.

Location: 1 mile (1.6km) south of Southwest Bay

Depth Range: 35-130ft+ (11-40m+)

Access: Boat

Expertise Rating: Intermediate

Divers explore Runway on zippy diver propulsion vehicles (DPVs).

The wall in this area is called Runway, for the New Providence airport runway north of the site. The name used to have a double meaning, referring to the number of large, winged southern stingrays that were once abundant in the area. The stingrays have departed for destinations unknown, but some small groups of Caribbean reef sharks have moved in to take their place. Runway starts around 70ft and gradually slopes down to 150ft before it hits a more vertical drop-off. Excellent hard corals and sponges are the rule on the face of the wall.

Shark Bowl is actually a collection of classic dive sites. Resident sharks in this area are fed on a regular basis, so divers will see sharks virtually every dive, even on regular dives when they are not being baited.

8 | Pumpkin Patch & Karen's Reef

These two sites lie on an unbroken stretch of pristine coral reef, which encompasses a shallow area (Karen's Reef) and a sloping wall (Pumpkin Patch). The sites are close enough together to visit on the same dive, but they are also often dived separately.

In the shallows, nice crops of various barrel, tube, pitted and rope sponges alternate with healthy hard corals. The wall is typified by sparser but still very healthy growth, including sheet corals and small orange elephant-ear sponges. There are always lots of fish at both sites,

Location: South of Southwest Bay

Depth Range: 25-130ft+ (7.6-40m+)

Access: Boat

Expertise Rating: Intermediate

including larger-than-normal numbers of the rare quillfin blenny. Friendly angelfish combine with schools of grunts and snappers and individual Nassau and tiger groupers.

Yellowtail snappers congregate near a shallow sponge formation at Pumpkin Patch.

9   Razorback & Playpen

Razorback is a great reef with varied topography. The reef's extremely healthy hard corals are adorned with rope sponges and purple tube sponges. Look for lots of angelfish, wrasses, Atlantic spadefish and more.

Razorback sits on the edge of the wall. On the reef's bank side you'll find a sand flat, home to stingrays, flounders and

Location: South of New Providence's west end

Depth Range: 40-130ft+ (12-40m+)

Access: Boat

Expertise Rating: Intermediate

Admiring Razorback's coral and sponge landscape.

garden eels. The sandy area slopes down to 65ft, where the reef begins. The name of the site comes from a sharp, distinct ridge that runs along the peak of the reef at 40ft. If you swim over the top or through a sand chute, you'll find yourself on the outer section of the reef, where it plunges into the depths.

Playpen is an adjacent site often explored in the same dive. This oval-shaped coral patch is encircled by a sand area featuring hordes of schooling fish, such as brown and blue chromis, French grunts, creole wrasses, lots of gobies and other small tropicals.

10   Southwest Reef

This expansive reef area features high-profile corals reaching nearly to the surface. Massive heads of star corals and huge branching elkhorn corals alternate with fire corals. All are decorated by purple sea fans and soft corals. Plenty of schooling fish, brilliantly colored tropicals and myriad invertebrates make this dive interesting even for experienced divers. With such rich shallow reef areas, Southwest Reef is ideal for the casual snorkeler. More-advanced free-divers

Location: South of western New Providence

Depth Range: 5-40ft (1.5-12m)

Access: Boat

Expertise Rating: Novice

and scuba divers will also find it excellent, especially for macrophotography.

11 Shark Wall, Shark Arena & *Edward Williams*

These three sites, each with a different environment, present the finest shark action available off New Providence. They sit close enough together that divers can easily explore all three in a single dive. This dive has become the premier New Providence experience for visiting divers, as well as for the several dozen sharks, primarily Caribbean reef and nurse sharks.

Location: 8 miles (13km) south along the Tongue of the Ocean

Depth Range: 30-130ft+ (9.1-40m+)

Access: Boat

Expertise Rating: Intermediate

Shark Wall is a beautiful sponge-draped wall. It's usually done as a first dive to acclimate divers to the presence of sharks. Sharks cruise around to investigate and compete with several large black groupers for your attention.

Divers kneel in the coral rubble as Caribbean reef sharks swim around at Shark Wall.

The actual shark feed happens at Shark Arena, a coral rubble patch in 45ft surrounded by coral reef that lies near the top of Shark Wall. Sharks begin to gather on the surface near the stern of the boat as soon as it's moored. Divers are arrayed in a half-circle with a safety diver nearby, while the feeders take their stations in front of them. The sharks here circulate in a rather orderly fashion as the feeder moderates the pace of the feed. You'll be within touching distance of the sharks, which cruise in and out of the feeding area.

The group of sharks in this area is primarily female, while the sharks found at Shark Bowl are mostly male. The behavior varies by gender—where the females tend to be orderly and less aggressive with one another, the males dart about more quickly and aggessively.

On the other side of Shark Arena is the *Edward Williams*, a decommissioned Bahamian Defense Force cutter. She lies in 45ft, topping out at around 30ft. The wreck has a coating of sessile invertebrates and is always visited by sharks.

A handler feeds a shark using a polespear.

12   Hole in the Head

At Hole in the Head, just south of Shark Arena, the 110ft shelf takes a broader turn than normal. Two massive coral heads are perched on this wide sandy ledge. The first rises from 110ft to 60ft and sports a tunnel running through it, lending the site its name. The second sits on the wall's edge and rises 20ft farther above the shelf, capping off just 40ft below the surface.

Location: 8 miles (13km) south along the Tongue of the Ocean

Depth Range: 40-130ft+ (12-40m+)

Access: Boat

Expertise Rating: Intermediate

The site's proximity to Shark Arena nearly guarantees the presence of sharks. Look for them resting inside the tunnel. All of the site's wall areas are covered with plate corals and tube sponges.

Look for coral and sponge formations and sharks during the journey through Hole in the Head.

13 The Graveyard (The Shipyard)

Their useful lives exhausted, three retired ships—the 150ft freighter *Ana Lise*, the 95ft *Helena C* and the 90ft *Bahama Shell*—were scuttled north of Paradise Island. The ships, which were downed between 1985 and 1992, have begun to develop a coating of coralline algae and encrusting sponges. That said, the waters north of New Providence do not promote the prolific growth you see to the south.

This underwater fleet is manned by angelfish, grunts, silversides, Atlantic spadefish and glassy sweepers. Larger visitors frequently swoop in unannounced.

Location: North of Paradise Island

Depth Range: 70-90ft (21-27m)

Access: Boat

Expertise Rating: Intermediate

Another nearby wreck, the **Mahoney**, was a victim of a natural disaster—the 1929 hurricane. Sitting in just 45ft, it lies broken in two pieces and sports lots of sponge growth. The *Mahoney* is too far away from the other wrecks to visit as part of the same dive.

14 De La Salle

Sitting upright in 70ft, the *De La Salle* rises about 20ft off the seafloor. Check inside her wheelhouse for barracuda and dog snappers and in her hold for grunts. You'll also usually see schools of sergeant

Location: Northwest of Salt Cay's west end

Depth Range: 50-70ft (15-21m)

Access: Boat

Expertise Rating: Intermediate

majors, as well as tangs and Bermuda chub. The outside of the wreck has developed a nice coating of sessile invertebrates, mostly coralline algae and encrusting sponges, along with the customary array of shrimp and other small invertebrates.

If you swim a short distance toward Salt Cay, you'll find a Haitian wooden sloop, the *Grennen*, in 60ft, and beyond that a small freighter, the *Miranda*, in 55ft. As is typical for wooden vessels, the *Grennen* is disintegrating rapidly.

15 | Fish Hotel

As the name implies, the big attraction at this site is fish, fish and more fish. French and blue-striped grunts intermingle, numbering in the thousands. You'll see the usual complement of French, gray and queen angelfish, porkfish, barracuda and many other tropicals.

The reef itself is fairly unexceptional—it's simply an uneven limestone bottom with potholes and ledges for shelter. The reef has few hard corals, but there are plenty of soft corals. Fish Hotel is a lesson in observation—put aside expectations of

Location: Off Salt Cay's east end

Depth Range: 16-24ft (4.9-7.3m)

Access: Boat

Expertise Rating: Novice

lush hard corals and you'll find plenty of intriguing items. Look in the corners and under ledges for crabs, moray eels and nurse sharks.

Massed of mixed grunts take up residence at Fish Hotel.

16 Barracuda Shoals

One of the prettiest reefs in the area, Barracuda Shoals is a triangle formed by three separate reef lines. The shallow site reaches to within 8ft of the surface and drops no deeper than 30ft.

Location: 12 miles (19km) east of New Providence's east end

Depth Range: 8-30ft (2.4-9.1m)

Access: Boat

Expertise Rating: Novice

Barracuda Shoals is vibrant with marine life.

Barracuda Shoals offers a very healthy assortment of hard corals, soft corals, sponges and fish. This balanced ecosystem is an ideal example of a good shallow Bahamian reef—rich coral and sponge formations awash in clear blue water host thickly schooling fish, as the strong rays of the sun dapple the clean white sand. Watch for green and chain morays, tiger and Nassau groupers and white- or orange-spotted filefish.

17 Lost Ocean Blue Hole

This dive site is a stunning example of a classic oceanic blue hole. It's an almost perfectly circular opening in the reef, which looks as clean as if it had been punched out by a cookie cutter. The lip of the hole sits between 40 and 60ft below the surface. The opening is broad, perhaps 120ft in diameter. From here this broad chimney drops vertically, providing a glimpse of the geologic history of The Bahamas.

Location: 10 miles (16km) east of New Providence's east end

Depth Range: 40-130ft+ (12-40m+)

Access: Boat

Expertise Rating: Intermediate

The area's marine life concentrates in and around this hole. Gray angelfish school in large numbers here, a behavior considered unusual. Big southern stingrays lie in the sand around the opening. Isolated, sponge-draped coral heads around the rim shelter groupers and snappers. Reef sharks sometimes retreat under the lip.

The hole drops to the peak of a debris cone at 180ft and bottoms out at 220ft, with tunnels leading into the substrate. A cavern sits on the east side, above a ledge at 80ft. Animal bones were reportedly discovered back in the deep tunnels.

Grand Bahama Dive Sites

At 85 miles (137km) long and 17 miles (27km) wide, Grand Bahama is large by Bahamian standards. It is the second-largest island in The Bahamas (the largest is Andros) and has about the same surface area as Great Abaco. Unfortunately, tourist and other commercial development has erased much of the charm characteristic of the Bahamian Out Islands. The focus of development and activity is in the Freeport/Port Lucaya area toward the west side of the island.

For those willing to venture away from the tourist areas, however, Grand Bahama still holds much to fascinate visitors. A road trip to the more remote east side will bring you through settlements steeped in the richer traditional Bahamian atmosphere. There are beautiful beaches, many of which seldom feel the touch of a human foot. The rarely visited north shore is a mass of mangroves and wetlands, a sanctuary for waterbirds and a nursery for juvenile fish and crustaceans. Several significant national parks—especially Lucayan National Park and Petersen Cay National Park—are definitely worth a visit.

The history of diving in Grand Bahama is tied closely to that of the Underwater Explorers Society (UNEXSO), a facility that opened its doors in 1964 and has hosted innumerable international diving heroes. UNEXSO, along with several

The Dolphin Experience program allows divers regular interactions with bottlenose dolphins.

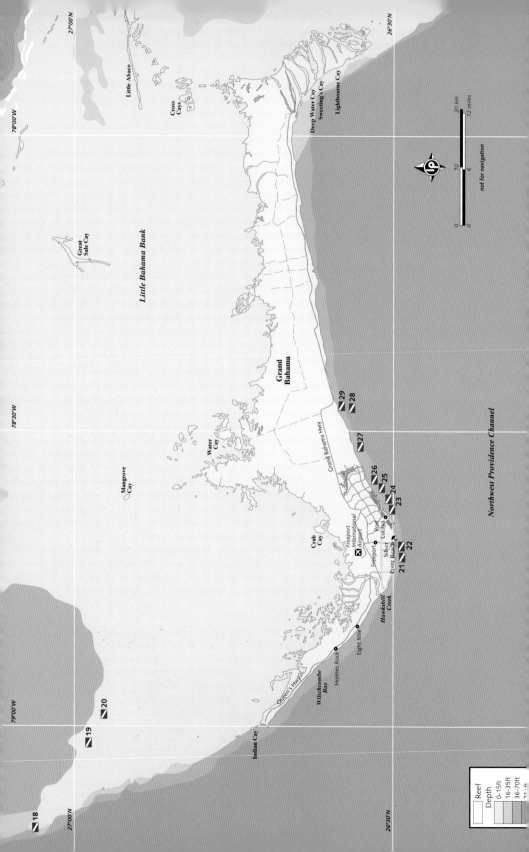

Little Abaco

Cross
Cays

Deep Water Cay
Sweeting's Cay
Lighthbourne Cay

Great
Sale Cay

Little Bahama Bank

27°00'N

78°00'W

78°30'W

Mangrove
Cay

Water
Cay

Grand
Bahama

29
28

Grand Bahama Hwy

27

Crab
Cay

Freeport
International
Airport

Freeport

Port

Lucaya

26
25
24
23

Silver
Point Beach

21
22

Hawksbill
Creek

Queen's Hwy

Wilstcombe
Bay

Holmes Rock

Eight Mile

Indian Cay

20

19

18

79°00'W

26°30'N

Northwest Providence Channel

not for navigation

20 km
12 miles

0   10
0   6

Reef

Depth
0-15ft
16-35ft
36-70ft
71 ft

other highly professional operations, affords divers dependable access to the best diving around Grand Bahama.

Dive sites are mostly concentrated along the south shore. They can generally be sorted by depth, as three levels of reef lines are clearly delineated. You'll find shallow reefs at less than 40ft (12m), moderate reefs between 40 and 60ft (12 and 18m) and deeper reefs, which include the edge of the wall. That said, wall diving along the sheer drops is not the main attraction in this area, as the walls tend to slope, becoming vertical only beyond accepted sport-diving limits.

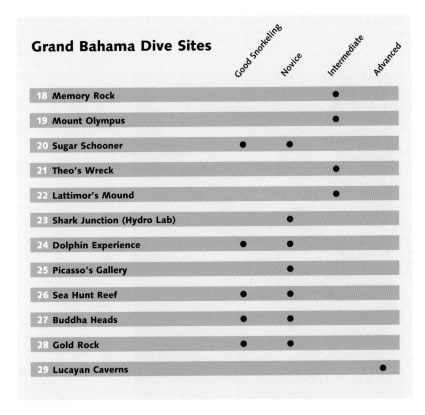

Grand Bahama Dive Sites	Good Snorkeling	Novice	Intermediate	Advanced
18 Memory Rock			●	
19 Mount Olympus			●	
20 Sugar Schooner	●	●		
21 Theo's Wreck			●	
22 Lattimor's Mound			●	
23 Shark Junction (Hydro Lab)		●		
24 Dolphin Experience	●	●		
25 Picasso's Gallery		●		
26 Sea Hunt Reef	●	●		
27 Buddha Heads	●	●		
28 Gold Rock	●	●		
29 Lucayan Caverns				●

Wallace Groves & the Bahamian Pine

The contemporary history of Grand Bahama has been largely defined by corporate lumbering. The lumber industry was chiefly created by Yankee financier and lumberman Wallace Groves, whose influence changed the face of the island forever. In the 1950s, Groves' interest was generated by the Bahamian Pine, a tall, close-grained and strong pine ideally suited to construction. In the raw forest, Groves envisioned wealth and a new city carved out of the virgin tracts of land. He had huge canals cut into the land, creating a system of inland waterways unparalleled in The Bahamas at the expense of the south shore reef system, which suffered from sedimentation.

18 | Memory Rock

Like the other Little Bahama Bank sites, Memory Rock is far enough from any land-based operation that it can only be dived by live-aboard. On the eastern edge of the Gulf Stream, the site is marked by name on nearly all nautical charts.

Memory Rock has the characteristics of the greatest Bahamian wall dives.

Location: 27 miles (43km) northwest of Grand Bahama's west end

Depth Range: 40-130ft+ (12-40m+)

Access: Live-aboard

Expertise Rating: Intermediate

Memory Rock's drop-off is draped with rich corals and sponges.

Spur-and-groove formations spill over the edge of a stair-stepped wall, which has deep grooves coursing through its face. Life on the wall is pure Bahamian beauty. Big sponges are the standard, including tube, stovepipe, barrel and basket sponges. Huge expanses of deepwater gorgonians and sparse growths of black corals cloak the sponges. As with any site situated directly in the path of the Gulf Stream, large pelagics are always a strong possibility.

The wall itself is very steep at its peak, and as you descend into the depths, it becomes both vertical and undercut. The various beach levels (formed by pauses in the rising and receding tides over the ages) usually found in The Bahamas are not as apparent here as on other walls.

19 | Mount Olympus

East of the wall, on the sand flats that fall into the Straits of Florida, Mount Olympus demonstrates the potential of a patch reef. The site consists of huge, rolling mounds of coral that climb from a sand base around 100ft and eventually peak at 50ft or less. This series of huge, interconnected coral heads is segmented by sand alleys. Divers can meander through the reef, climbing up slopes and then gliding down them to the valleys below. Stingrays and turtles will be your favored companions.

Location: 12 miles (32km) north of Grand Bahama's west end

Depth Range: 50-100ft (15-30m)

Access: Live-aboard

Expertise Rating: Intermediate

Deepwater gorgonians form undulating curtains across the prominent coral heads. You are almost certain to spot southern stingrays either buried in the sand or swimming within the ravines and crevices of the reef. Orange elephant-ear sponges perch on the edge of the reef. The fish life is varied—cleaning gobies host cleaning stations, moray eels entwine themselves in the honeycombed reef, and several varieties of grouper and parrotfish rest under the many ledges.

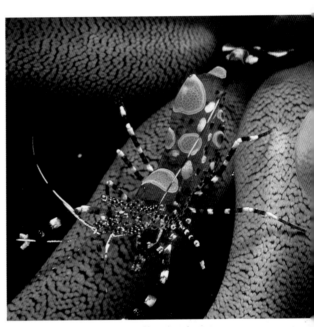

This tiny cleaner shrimp lives in the arms of a sea anemone.

20 | Sugar Schooner

Sugar Schooner is named for a vessel that carried a load of raw sugar, which found its final resting place on the Little Bahama Bank, just miles from the deep waters of the Gulf Stream. Now thoroughly flattened and spread out over a large area of seafloor, this unidentified wreck has made a fruitful home for many marine creatures.

Location: 2 miles (3.2km) inside the Little Bahama Bank

Depth Range: 12-20ft (3.7-6m)

Access: Live-aboard

Expertise Rating: Novice

Notable residents include a large great barracuda and many fully mature green and loggerhead sea turtles, which find this site a perfect night-time resting place. The site is a popular nighttime anchorage for live-aboards and thus for night dives, when the turtles are the stars of the scene. A peek under a section of plating may reveal a nurse shark and a green turtle resting side by side. The wreck's remnants also host large numbers of colonial tunicates, along with other sessile invertebrates.

A school of grunts passes through the Sugar Schooner.

21 Theo's Wreck

Theo's Wreck is one of the finest and most-dived wrecks in The Bahamas. She rests on her side in a maximum of 110ft at the stern, a short distance from the edge of the drop-off into the Southwest Providence Channel.

When she first slid off the blocks into Norway's icy waters in 1954, this vessel was christened the MS *Logna*. When her hull was washed by the warm waters of her new home, The Bahamas, she was renamed the MV *Island Cement*. Finally, when her useful life was finally spent and she was ready to be scrapped, Theodopolis Galanoupoulos, an engineer and manager at the cement company that owned her, came up with the brilliant idea to give her new life as a divers' playground. On October 16, 1982, with the help of UNEXSO, Theo's Wreck slipped beneath the waves and became part of Grand Bahama's marine heritage.

In her two decades underwater, the wreck has become an oasis for marine

Location: South of the Silver Point Beach inlet

Depth Range: 70-110ft (21-34m)

Access: Boat

Expertise Rating: Intermediate

life. Her hull appears deceptively clean, but shine a light on it and you will be rewarded with an explosion of color. Yellow and orange cup corals and pink and red encrusting sponges mix with lavender and purple calcareous algaes. Tunicates and hydroids carpet the hull and hang off the rails and anchor chains.

Residents include a large and somewhat gregarious green moray, barracuda, parrotfish, angelfish, snappers and grunts. The wreck's proximity to the drop-off invites inquiring visits by turtles and larger fish. Check the sand near the stern for yellowhead jawfish burrowing in the sand.

The ship was well prepared for penetration, and its cargo holds stand open and inviting. The Bahamas National Trust has declared Theo's Wreck a National Heritage Site, and as such she is protected. She gets better with each passing year.

A diver swims above Theo's Wreck, one of Grand Bahama's premier dive sites.

22 Lattimor's Mound

Many local dive operators consider Lattimor's Mound to be one of the very best medium-depth reefs in this area. This site consists of a single huge, segmented coral mound. Since the surrounding plain is a combination of sand and rubble, you'll find a variety of life suited to either one environment or the other. Look for shy garden eels in the fine sand bottom or yellowhead jawfish in the rougher rubble bottom.

Location: West of Silver Point Channel

Depth Range: 52-70ft (16-21m)

Access: Boat

Expertise Rating: Intermediate

Expect to find squirrelfish, hamlets, glasseye snappers and other reticent reef dwellers. The hard corals here are sheet corals (morphs of star corals). These combine with some deepwater soft corals.

Squirrelfish are common on shallow reefs and wall tops throughout The Bahamas.

23 Shark Junction (Hydro Lab)

Shark Junction registers high on the Bahamian shark scale. All feeders, safety divers and videographers wear chain mail shark suits. Guests are positioned with their backs to a decommissioned recompression chamber on the site. Shark Junction is a high-energy but well-controlled dive, as good as any shark dive in The Bahamas.

Location: South of the Bell Channel entrance to Port Lucaya

Depth: 50ft (15m)

Access: Boat

Expertise Rating: Novice

It was here that feeders first began handling Caribbean reef sharks. Less

This shark isn't as menacing as it seems—it's simply inhaling a fish released from the feeder's hand.

than a decade ago Ben Rose, a well-known (some would say notorious) local dive guide, first warmed up to kissing a shark. Rose had no idea how the shark would react to this unprecedented advance.

During the decade after Rose first succeeded in his intimate encounter, shark wranglers here have refined their interactions to the point that they can literally place a shark in a trance, stroking its snout and holding the

fierce creature's head in their laps. The wrangler can pick the animal up by its dorsal fin and head and bring it around to give visiting divers a close-up look at this extraordinary predator. After it's released, the shark simply shakes its head, takes a lingering glance around and slowly swims off.

This site is also home to UNEXSO's Shark Feeder program. This closely supervised multi-day course allows guests to become part of the action.

24 Dolphin Experience

Few experiences can compare with swimming with a dolphin in the open ocean. The curiosity, playfulness, intelligence and open sense of fun shared by both human and dolphin make for a unique dynamic. The problem? How to plan these encounters. Atlantic spotted dolphins tend to be both gregarious and predictable in their habits. But when it comes to bottlenose dolphins encountered in the open ocean, the exchanges tend to be short-lived. Over the past decade or so, UNEXSO (one of the most

Location: 1 mile (1.6km) south of Sanctuary Bay

Depth Range: 50ft (15m)

Access: Boat

Expertise Rating: Novice

complete dive operations in The Bahamas) has developed a program that allows divers a reliable way to interact with bottlenose dolphins.

An offshoot of the UNEXSO dive operation, the Dolphin Experience program is devoted to raising dolphins in captivity and acclimating them to exchanges with humans. This is one of only two programs in the Caribbean in which dolphins swim to the open ocean to interact with snorkelers and divers. In contrast with dolphin shows, which are strictly about entertainment, the UNEXSO program places a heavy emphasis on education. The animals are captive, but only to a degree—the fences at Sanctuary Bay are low enough for the dolphins to leave if they choose. The dolphins stick around.

On Dolphin Flats, the actual open-ocean site, dolphins (usually two on each dive) approach from any direction. Take your regulator out of your mouth and they will expect a kiss from you. The site is close to Shark Junction, so the dolphins do get

A pair of bottlenose dolphins befriends a diver.

spooked by the sharks from time to time, hightailing it back to Sanctuary Bay. The program also features lectures, petting from a water-level platform and snorkeling in the bay. There are currently a dozen dolphins in Sanctuary Bay, and attempts at breeding in captivity have proven successful.

A Date with a Dolphin

Dolphins are perhaps the most beloved of marine animals. Many people connect profoundly with the mammals' playfulness, responsiveness, affection and the seeming awareness and intelligence in their eyes. While some experts believe affixing human qualities to dolphins is a mistake, others are convinced if dolphins had thumbs, they would rule the world. In either case, sharing time in the ocean with dolphins is an extraordinary experience.

In The Bahamas virtually all encounters happen with one of the two primary species—the bottlenose dolphin (*Tursiops truncatus*) and the Atlantic spotted dolphin (*Stenella frontalis*). The gregarious Atlantic spotted dolphin tends to allow a greater degree of in-water interaction than the more wary bottlenose species. In several areas around The Bahamas, encounters with spotted dolphins in the wild occur on a dependably regular basis. The most famous spot is **White Sand Ridge** on the western edge of the Little Bahama Bank, north of Grand Bahama. For many years the spot was a secret known only to sailors and boaters, but the past decade has seen the secret shared with the world at large.

Alerted by the sound of a boat's engines, the dolphins (as many as a dozen per pod) come swimming and leaping next to the boat, as if inviting passengers into the water. You'll get more out of the experience if you use only snorkel gear. It's not the sound of the bubbles that dampens the experience, rather it is simply that the dolphins like to play. Without gear you are more agile and more interesting to them. If you are a passable freediver, you can try diving down and swimming with the dolphins in their own environment. The more entertaining you are, the more they will stay with you, circling, swimming and clicking happily. It's fascinating to watch them mimic divers—try doing a dolphin kick and watch as they exaggerate their own swimming motions, like it's an inside joke.

Because of White Sand Ridge's open-water position and its variable winter weather conditions, the peak time to visit is between April and September. The ridge is far away from land-based dive operations, so it is normally visited only by live-aboard dive vessels.

Another pod frequents the waters off Orange Cay, near the south end of the Bimini chain. This area is accessible by live-aboard only. In another area off Bimini's northern coast that is accessible by day boats, a different pod has taken up residence. Divers encounter this pod almost daily, usually in the late afternoon. Check with Bimini operators—they have made this a standard part of their dive activities.

25 Picasso's Gallery

Picasso's Gallery consists of isolated coral heads in shallow water. Many of these heads do not exhibit all-encompassing live growth, but rather have relatively recent top growth over the skeletal limestone structure of their ancestors. As the bottom slopes down into deeper waters, these separate coral heads gradually merge into a solid reef.

While algal overgrowth is as much a problem here as it is nearly everywhere, the strength of the coral growth tends to overshadow this visually. Algae may

Location: East of Sanctuary Bay

Depth Range: 32-50ft (9.8-15m)

Access: Boat

Expertise Rating: Novice

overgrow a reef in the absence of algal feeders such as sea urchins. This problem plagues all Caribbean reefs. It is still a fine dive, as invertebrate life is strong and there is an abundance of smaller tropical fish.

26 Sea Hunt Reef

An echo of the past, Sea Hunt Reef was the location for much of the underwater filming for the television series of

Location: Just east of Sanctuary Bay

Depth Range: 6-20ft (1.8-6m)

Access: Boat

Expertise Rating: Novice

the same name. Mike Nelson (played by Lloyd Bridges) entertained us through the 1950s, battling nefarious villains underwater. The bad guys inevitably severed the exhaust hose of his two-hose regulator, making for dramatic and bubble-filled scenes. These moments embedded this reef into the subconscious of the world. Rolling off the side of the boat and working alone, Mike Nelson was the epitome of diver cool at a time when sport diving was in its infancy. By the way, Lloyd Bridges was one of the charter members of UNEXSO.

Today this shallow reef still delivers an array of isolated coral heads, each sustaining and protecting its own colony of fish. As with many sites in this area, soft corals atop the largely extinct hard corals add texture, motion and color to a somewhat drab reef. The reef features other sessile invertebrates, schooling fish and the flashing colors of small tropicals.

27 Buddha Heads

The name Buddha Heads can probably be attributed to the broad but diminutive stature of the coral heads strewn across the hardscrabble seafloor. As with many sites southeast of Grand Bahama, they are beyond the normal reach of day boats but are done upon request and are well worth the extra time.

Location: East of Lucaya Waterway outlet

Depth Range: 28-43ft (8.5-13m)

Access: Boat

Expertise Rating: Novice

As with many Grand Bahama sites, much of the topographic interest at this site is due to the presence of soft corals such as sea rods and sea plumes. Photographers will find the low-lying reef unexceptional, but the fish life is very good. The primary focus should be on fish and invertebrate portraits, but there are larger animals to watch, including rays and nurse sharks.

Goatfish use the pair of barbels below their chin to dig in the sand for food.

28 Gold Rock

Gold Rock is a beautiful shallow reef featuring a large number of tightly packed but separate coral heads joined by limestone ridges. The ridges (spurs) run seaward, a classic example of a spur-and-groove reef.

Location: South of central Grand Bahama

Depth Range: 28-45ft (8.5-14m)

Access: Boat

Expertise Rating: Novice

Banded butterflyfish are common reef dwellers.

Lots of sea fans and sea whips adorn the upper reaches of the hard corals. Some tall and very nice examples of the relatively unusual pillar coral are found here. The mid-water is filled with brown and blue chromis, while squirrelfish and bigeyes peek out from every crevice. Check the rubble areas for sand tilefish.

29 Lucayan Caverns

Initially explored by local dive guide Ben Rose, this extensive cavern and cave system is the largest and best-mapped in The Bahamas. More than 6 miles of line have been laid in these tunnels, which sit within the boundaries of Lucayan National Park. Two separate openings lead into the cavern system. The water level lies lower than the openings to the caves and steps lead down to the waterline.

Location: South of central Grand Bahama

Depth Range: Surface-40ft (12m)

Access: Shore

Expertise Rating: Advanced

The surrounding acres of the park hold an ecologically and culturally rich area well worth taking time to explore. Bats sleep in the cool caves in the heat of the day. Several types of indigenous marine life are found here. Several sightless cave-dwelling fish and invertebrates live in the waters.

Dives in **Ben's Cave** must be scheduled in advance. Due to the fragile nature of the environment, groups are limited to four divers, and only a certain number of divers are allowed to access the site each year.

In 1986 four Lucayan skeletons were discovered in the section of the system known as **Burial Mound Cave**, lending credence to the idea that this protected area was used as an Indian burial ground when water levels were lower.

At Gold Rock, a pillar coral formation—relatively unusual in The Bahamas—attracts copious fish life.

At the northwest corner of the Great Bahama Bank, Bimini is known for its reefs, big fish and freewheeling spirit. Though it sits only 48 miles (77km) from Miami—close enough that you can listen to Miami radio—Bimini maintains the air of a removed Out Island. The island group has long possessed a wildly rustic and fiercely independent frontier reputation. When Ernest Hemingway wrote *Islands in the Stream*, he was recalling his days spent fishing, drinking and brawling in Bimini in the 1930s. He lived at the Compleat Angler, in Room 1 at the top of the stairs, where he made a standing offer to whip anyone who wanted to take him on. Today a wealth of photos decorating the walls of the Angler form a shrine to him.

What is commonly called Bimini is actually the northern (and better-known) of two main islands—North and South Bimini are divided by a narrow channel. On North Bimini a narrow strip of land forms the west side of Porgy Bay. It stretches 7 miles (11km) north from Alice Town, reaching a maximum width of just 700ft (213m). At the northern point it doglegs back to an expansive mangrove area.

Much as it has for decades, the Compleat Angler offers up cool libations and simple meals.

Most visitors arrive via seaplane, landing in the calm water of North Bimini's backcountry. There is an airstrip for small planes on South Bimini. Though largely undeveloped, South Bimini does have at least one establishment devoted to diving. Alice Town on North Bimini is the center of activity. Only two roads—really just narrow sandy lanes—pass through Alice Town, optimistically named the Queen's and the King's Highways. A five-minute stroll across town will take you past Alice Town's colorful assortment of funky bars, unassuming shops and little restaurants.

Bimini's shores are washed by the Gulf Stream as it flows north through the Straits of Florida. This, combined with the expansive flats, gives Bimini an outstanding variety of marine life. Reef activity is prolific, and Bimini is known as one of the fishiest of all the islands. Watch for spotted eagle rays passing through the channel between the islands as they feed—dozens fly by on almost any given day. The Gulf Stream throws large pelagics into the mix—it's not unusual to sight sharks or larger game fish. With one notable exception, wall diving is not the primary attraction around Bimini.

Wrecking & Smuggling

It's late at night in The Bahamas, and a small gale is blowing on the Gulf Stream. Locals wait on the edge of the offshore reef, hanging lanterns to swing in the screaming wind, outlining the shallowest, most treacherous portions of the limestone reef. Offshore, a ship making its way through the storm posts a lookout in the crow's nest, who peers through the curtains of rain, desperately seeking shelter. The lights appear to be other ships at anchor, a signal that secure anchorage is at hand. With a sigh of relief, the crew gamely prepares to secure the vessel. Within minutes the vessel's bottom has been ripped out by the ragged teeth of the reef, crewmembers are fighting for their lives and the Bahamians are congratulating themselves on yet another prize.

This practice was known as wrecking and reaches back to the earliest Bahamian settlers. International Admiralty Law allowed a great degree of latitude in what was allowed in the name of salvage. A wrecked ship was considered abandoned the moment the last person stepped off its deck, at which time the ship and its cargo became fair game. The first person to step aboard acquired salvage rights. A legal form of thievery, wrecking was a direct descendant of piracy, privateering and the loose laws of the high seas. It was also considered a valid way to provide for one's family and community.

This unscrupulous attitude is an essential part of the Bahamian tradition. It stems from the islands' early settlers, a motley crew of shipwrecked sailors, marooned pirates, escaped slaves, wanderers and adventurers, loners and lovelorn castoffs. The tradition of wrecking evolved into other, more-current traditions that sidestep the law. At the very top of the list is smuggling. With the Florida coast just a short hop away, smuggling can be a profitable and relatively safe endeavor. What the United States wants but prohibits, The Bahamas will deliver. The most famous historical example is rum-running during the 1920s Prohibition era, when daily shipments of rum, Irish whiskey and other liquors made their way onto American shores. This tradition continues in the form of drug trafficking, principally out the west end of Grand Bahama, Bimini and the islands of the Bimini chain.

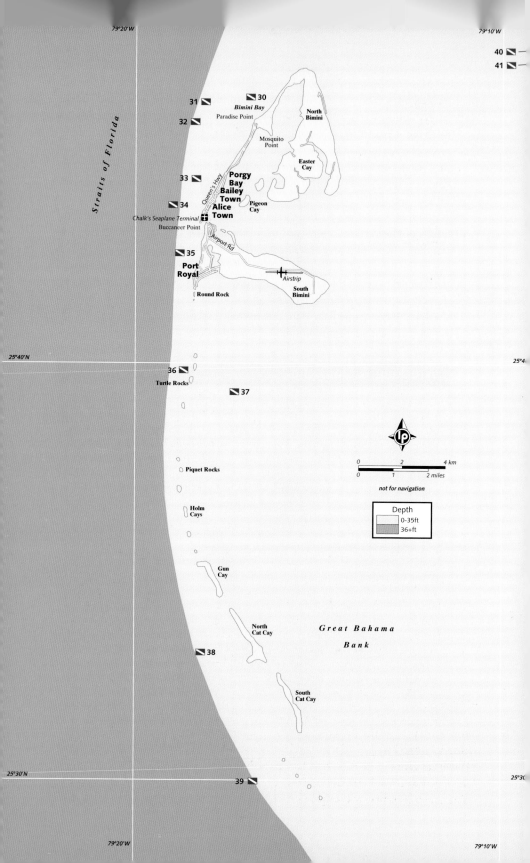

Bimini Dive Sites

		Good Snorkeling	Novice	Intermediate	Advanced
30	**The Bimini Road (Road to Atlantis)**	●	●		
31	**Hawksbill Reef**		●		
32	**Little Caverns**			●	
33	**The Strip**	●	●		
34	**The Wall**			●	
35	**Bimini Barge**			●	
36	**Turtle Rocks**	●	●		
37	*Sapona*	●	●		
38	**Tuna Alley**			●	
39	**The Victories**			●	
40	*Hesperus*	●	●		
41	**Gingerbread Grounds**	●	●		

30 The Bimini Road (Road to Atlantis)

At first glance The Bimini Road is rather unimposing as a dive site. Growth on the limestone floor is sparse, and few fish occupy the open terrain. The site's main interest is a double line of huge square blocks, which seem to be man-made and intentionally placed. Each line is nearly 75 yards long, made up of blocks about 6ft square.

There are many who believe the stones may be remnants of the legendary lost civilization of Atlantis. The debate concerning its origins—whether the structure is manmade or is the result of natural phenomena—is ongoing. The

Location: ¼ mile (.4km) northwest of North Point

Depth Range: 20-25ft (6-7.6m)

Access: Boat

Expertise Rating: Novice

usual standard rule is that there are no straight lines in nature, but these square limestone blocks are neatly arranged in two perfect lines. They certainly seem like a sign of some unrecorded civilization.

Bimini Mysteries

The Bermuda Triangle, echoes of Atlantis, mysterious Indian mounds, healing forces, energy vortexes and interdimensional portals—all have been associated with Bimini. Hocus-pocus? Perhaps, but for some reason Bimini has attracted a great deal of attention for its perceived metaphysical and spiritual characteristics.

The Bimini mystique is not a recent phenomenon. The ancient Lucayans believed in the spiritual powers of water drawn from a particular spring on South Bimini. It was said that its waters made the old young and the sick well. In 1513, Spanish explorer Ponce de León wandered the archipelago in search of this spring, believing it to be the fabled Fountain of Youth. Even today there are those who swear by its powers.

The Fountain of Youth has a counterpart in the mangroves of North Bimini. A boat ride across the backwaters and a short wade down a canal brings you to a small, spring-fed lagoon known as the Healing Hole. Again, the Lucayans honored this location. Today residents and visitors who soak in these waters swear by their medicinal powers. Analysis of the water bubbling up from this freshwater sulphur spring does show a higher-than-normal mineral content and a high lithium content.

Not far away from the Healing Hole is a series of earthen mounds believed to be Indian mounds. Some exceed 500ft (152m) in length. They look nondescript from sea level, but from the air they have distinct shapes: a seahorse, a shark, a cat and various geometric forms. Some believe the mounds were signals to extraterrestrial beings.

The Bimini Islands sit at the southwest corner of the infamous Bermuda Triangle. Any number of local disappearances have been recorded, but the most famous incident was the loss of five Grumman Avenger bombers on a training run out of Fort Lauderdale in 1945. Their destination was Hens and Chicken, a shoal 22 miles (35km) north of the Biminis. After a routine run, something happened. All pilots became disoriented, their compasses started spinning wildly and, in time, all communication was disrupted. None of the planes returned to port, and no wreckage was ever found. What happened remains a mystery, but believers are convinced the planes disappeared into some kind of an interdimensional portal.

The Biminis's biggest claim to fame, however, is the Bimini Road, an underwater formation believed by some to be evidence of the lost civilization of Atlantis. Divers can visit the site and examine the two parallel lines of large square blocks. Because straight lines are very rare in nature—especially multiple repeats like this—these stones have every appearance of being manmade, both in shape and in arrangement. The road's legendary status is highlighted by an uncanny fact—in the late 1930s famed psychic Edgar Cayce predicted that evidence of Atlantis would rise near Bimini in 1969. Oddly enough, it was in 1969 that the pilot of a low-flying plane first caught sight of this unusual formation beneath the waters off Bimini. Doubters claim coincidence, but others take this as evidence that the road is a focus of Atlantean energy.

A more scientific explanation may be that they are made of beach rock, which as it dries and shrinks tends to break at right angles.

Some say the stones of the Bimini Road are evidence of the lost civilization of Atlantis.

31 Hawksbill Reef

Hawksbill Reef is a perennial Bimini favorite. The site covers a large area and has three separate moorings. Low-lying corals shaped like popcorn kernels split the bottom about fifty-fifty with sandy patches.

The mid-water always features large schools of Bermuda chub. Medium-sized Nassau groupers are usually found here, and massive schools of snappers and grunts are the rule. Keep an eye open for

Location: 1.4 miles (2.3km) northwest of Porgy Bay

Depth Range: 35-47ft (11-14m)

Access: Boat

Expertise Rating: Novice

stingrays and nurse sharks and look in the sand for yellowhead jawfish and tile-fish. Large schools of baitfish provide a year-round food supply for larger fish.

32 Little Caverns

Little Caverns is one Bimini's best deep reefs. This area offers thickly packed, 10- to 20ft-tall coral heads, which have in some cases grown together to form small swim-throughs. The heads are decorated with sea fans and sponges, including large and nicely formed basket, barrel and tube sponges, as well as numerous encrusting varieties.

Large groupers are common, as are queen and gray angelfish, spotted eagle

Location: 1.4 miles (2.3km) northwest of Porgy Bay

Depth Range: 60-84ft (18-26m)

Access: Boat

Expertise Rating: Intermediate

rays, southern stingrays and schools of snappers and Bermuda chub. The reef is frequented by nurse sharks, with occasional visits from their bigger brothers.

Schoolmasters and other reef fish take shelter in the many small holes at Little Caverns.

33 The Strip

Bimini's number one night dive is The Strip, a long thin reef in the middle of a sandy area. Lying in 35ft of water, the reef is about 600ft long and only about 20ft wide. The reef's unusual shape makes nighttime navigation easy.

Because this is the only reef in the immediate area, marine life tends to concentrate here. The Strip hosts schools of black margates, squirrelfish and mixed schools of grunts, as well as green morays

Location: Midway up North Bimini

Depth Range: 30-35ft (9.1-11m)

Access: Boat

Expertise Rating: Novice

and other eels. Nighttime brings out reef crabs, octopuses and more.

A diver comes face to face with a large reef crab on a night dive at The Strip.

34 The Wall

This drift dive is not to be missed—it's a well-orchestrated, eight-minute trip in the Gulf Stream, which brings you over the edge of the Bahamian shelf.

After the boat is positioned above the edge of the wall, the crew drops a weighted 130ft line over the side. On a signal from the divemaster, all divers roll over the edge of the boat, connect

Location: West of North Bimini's southern tip

Depth Range: 100-130ft+ (30-40m+)

Access: Boat

Expertise Rating: Intermediate

with the line and descend to between 100 and 130ft.

The wall starts deep, at 145 to 165ft. You drift for eight minutes, watching the drop-off unfold below you. Sponges as large as any you've ever seen perch pre-cariously on the edge of the precipice. Watch for large sharks and eagle rays. A three-minute hang at 15ft completes the dive. Be sure to keep an eye on the blue water—you never know what may come sailing out of the dark.

35 Bimini Barge

Bimini's premier wreck dive is the Bimini Barge. This 150ft oceangoing barge sat at a dock for years before it was quietly scuttled sometime in 1986 or '87. The wreck sat unknown until it was relocated by Bimini dive operator Bill Keefe in June 1990.

The barge sits upright in 85 to 95ft. Its deck lies at 75ft and its highest point reaches to 65ft. The wreck is situated near the edge of the drop-off, so you should expect to see some big fish. Large black groupers, amberjack and schooling barracuda are common. Check under the

Location: Outside the cut between North and South Bimini

Depth Range: 65-95ft (20-29m)

Access: Boat

Expertise Rating: Intermediate

stern for 5 to 6ft southern stingrays and keep an eye open for schooling permits. Though the current can make this dive a challenge, it's well worth the effort.

The Bimini Barge, Bimini's finest wreck, is washed by currents near the edge of the wall.

36 Turtle Rocks

Several rocks protrude from the water just south of Bimini—these are called North Turtle Rock, Middle Turtle Rock and South Turtle Rock.

The Turtle Rocks dive site is a reef bordering the west side of these rocks. Sloping down from the surface, the reef is made up of rock ledges and isolated coral heads.

Location: 2.2 miles (3.5km) south of South Bimini

Depth Range: Surface-35ft (11m)

Access: Boat

Expertise Rating: Novice

Glassy sweepers crowd under a shallow ledge at Turtle Rocks.

Middle Turtle Rocks has one massive star-coral head that towers above the rest, rising perhaps 20ft from the bottom. The grunts school so thickly here that they virtually cover the smaller coral heads. Look beneath the ledges for swirling schools of glassy sweepers, nurse sharks and the occasional resting turtle. Southern sting-rays are abundant in the sand flats, while spotted eagle rays often hover above the bottom. Every once in a while, a large pelagic will come swooping in from deep water, take a quick look around and depart as quickly as it appeared.

37 *Sapona*

The Liberty Ship *Sapona* is a ferro-cement vessel built in 1904 by Miami developer Henry Flagler. The ship came to Bimini to be used as a floating night-club and casino, but a 1926 hurricane blew her aground on the banks behind Turtle Rocks. In the years that followed, the wrecked vessel served as a holding tank for liquor being smuggled to the United States, a late-night party location and a target for U.S. bombing and straf-ing runs.

Sitting half in and half out of the water, the *Sapona* presents divers and snorkelers a fascinating intersection of the underwater and topside realms. The

Location: On the bank southwest of Turtle Rocks

Depth Range: Surface-12ft (3.7m)

Access: Boat

Expertise Rating: Novice

hull is filled with and surrounded by schools of grunts and blackbar soldier-fish, while nurse sharks patrol the perimeter. For photographers, the wide-angle possibilities compete fiercely with the macro potential of the wreck.

Half in the water and half out, the *Sapona* attracts divers, snorkelers and plenty of fish life.

38 Tuna Alley

Tuna Alley is named for the annual northerly migration of giant 400 to 800lb bluefin tuna. The migration starts in mid-April and lasts until early June. Great hammerhead sharks follow this migration, nipping at the outside of the pack, so shark sightings are far more frequent at this time.

Location: Northwest of South Cat Cay

Depth Range: 40-130ft+ (12-40m+)

Access: Boat

Expertise Rating: Intermediate

Here a sloping wall drops to a sand shelf at 120ft, rising up in a second ridge to about 70ft and then taking a more severe angle into the depths of the Straits of Florida. Most of the diving on Tuna Alley is done between 55 and 95ft. Corals are a feature of this dive—on a single visit you can spot growths of feather, orange sea fan, bushy and bottlebrush black corals.

Tuna Alley stretches for nearly 7 miles and has a half-dozen separate moorings, some for day boats and others for larger liveaboard vessels. Due to the proximity of the Gulf Stream, you should expect some strong currents.

Clouds of swirling silversides seasonally fill the holes in the reef at Tuna Alley.

39 The Victories

The reefs in this area are ancient spur-and-groove formations. The lines have grown together many times, forming deep-cut crevices and canyons, as well as elaborate systems of tunnels and arches.

Location: West of Victory Cay

Depth Range: 40-85ft (12-26m)

Access: Boat

Expertise Rating: Intermediate

The Victories reef system is filled with caverns.

These skeletal formations are overlaid with a broad representation of Caribbean corals. Nearly every available surface that isn't occupied by live coral growth is heavily encrusted with a wildly colorful profusion of filter-feeders. Dark volcano sponges, considered rare elsewhere, grow in abundance. Tangled masses of rope and finger sponges compete for space with tunicates and gorgonians.

The wall drops at a slope to a sand shelf at about 90ft. This shelf continues to slope for a couple of hundred yards before finally dropping into the abyss. The best diving is found on the sloping walls above this shelf, in depths ranging from 35 to 85ft. Keep your eyes open and expect the unexpected, as the blue waters of the Gulf Stream can bring in nearly anything. Be prepared for the possibility of strong currents.

40 Hesperus

The *Hesperus* is a small wreck whose origin is somewhat hazy. It is believed to have been an interisland freighter that foundered in a storm in the mid-1950s. The *Hesperus* was not the craft's original name.

The wreck is rather broken-up, but its remains shelter huge numbers of angel-fish and schooling French, smallmouth

Location: 25 miles (40km) northeast of Bimini

Depth Range: 12-20ft (3.7-6m)

Access: Live-aboard

Expertise Rating: Novice

and striped grunts. The site's biggest attraction, however, is the abundance of resident turtles. They tend to be out foraging during the day, but at night at least a dozen huge turtles sleep on the wreck.

You can sit on the dive platform and watch these large green and loggerhead turtles rise to the surface, breathe noisily and slowly slip away, quietly dropping below the surface of the water.

Schools of mixed grunts wrap around the remains of the *Hesperus*.

41 Gingerbread Grounds

This expansive reef area spreads across acres of ocean floor. It's out of reach of daytrips but is visited regularly by live-aboards.

High-profile coral heads, reaching 25ft or more off the bottom, have deep undercuts and ledges that shelter masses of orange cup corals, white telesto corals and a greater variety of tunicates than almost any other site in The Bahamas. Schooling gray snappers are very common, as are good-sized lobsters and reef

Location: 34 miles (54km) northeast of Bimini

Depth Range: 15-45ft (4.6-14m)

Access: Live-aboard

Expertise Rating: Novice

crabs. Nurse sharks are seen frequently in the sand patches, as are stingrays.

Berry Islands Dive Sites

Just 17 miles (27km) north of Andros and 30 miles (48km) northwest of New Providence, this chain of about 30 low-lying limestone and sand spits spans more than 30 miles (48km). Over the centuries, the Berry Islands have seen very little sustained human settlement. Today they are still very sparsely settled, with

A diver explores a coral formation dripping with brilliant yellow sponges.

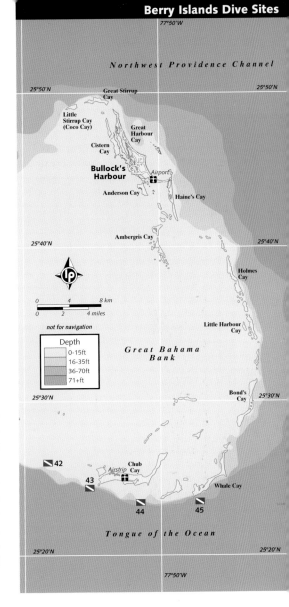

a total population of less than a thousand. From time to time the islands function as a getaway for the rich and famous but are otherwise very quiet. Cruise lines share ownership of Great and Little Stirrup Cays (they renamed the latter Coco Cay), and one day a week cruisers quadruple the islands' population.

Great Harbour Cay is the focus of local activity. On most of the islands your main options are fishing and diving. Bonefishing on the flats to the west is excellent, as is billfishing in the deep waters of the Northwest Providence Channel to the south.

Diving activity is focused around Chub Cay and its neighboring islands in the southern portion of the chain. Although the north offers good spur-and-groove formations, weather conditions make diving difficult. In the south you can almost always find a favorable lee for diving the walls and shallow patch reefs.

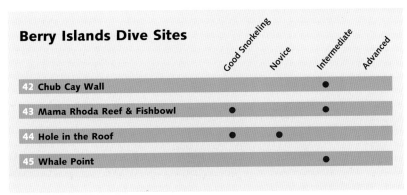

Berry Islands Dive Sites

	Good Snorkeling	Novice	Intermediate	Advanced
42 Chub Cay Wall			●	
43 Mama Rhoda Reef & Fishbowl	●		●	
44 Hole in the Roof	●	●		
45 Whale Point			●	

42 Chub Cay Wall

The mooring for Chub Cay Wall is in the center of a long stretch of steeply sloping to nearly vertical wall, with many overhangs and tunnels. Sheet corals create many of the overhangs where they have grown out and protrude off the face of the wall. Stands of bushy black corals and wire corals are intertwined with deep-water sea fans and other gorgonians.

Pelagics, especially spotted eagle rays, often cruise by. Sightings of wandering pods of pilot whales are also frequently

Location: 5 miles (8km) west of Mama Rhoda Rock

Depth Range: 60-130ft+ (18-40m+)

Access: Boat

Expertise Rating: Intermediate

reported. Look for blackcap basslets on the deeper sections of the wall.

The wall at the south end of the Berry Islands boasts huge coral and sponge growths.

43 | Mama Rhoda Reef & Fishbowl

Location: South side of Mama Rhoda Rock

Depth Range: 5-130ft+ (1.5-40m+)

Access: Boat

Expertise Rating: Intermediate

Mama Rhoda Reef is a great little snorkeling reef spread over a large expanse of ocean floor. It offers excellent potential for fish-watching and macrophotography. Sea plumes and sea fans sway in the light surge as big schools of various snappers and grunts shelter in the arms of the elkhorn and staghorn corals. As with any shallow reef in the hurricane zone, these shallow-water corals come and go. They grow very quickly and tend to recover rapidly from storm damage. You'll also find a variety of rays, some nurse sharks and a surprisingly large number of nudibranchs.

South of Mama Rhoda Reef you'll find Fishbowl, a steeply sloping wall site made up of sand gullies and high-profile spurs that join together at their peaks to form arches. The face of the wall is a profusion of color, featuring a broad variety of sponges. Masses of rope sponges hang over large elephant-ear and barrel sponges.

As you might guess from the name, the fish life is very good. Snappers school while jacks circle in the mid-water. Look on the surfaces of the sponges and corals for unusual tropicals, such as arrow and triplefin blennies.

A large orange elephant-ear sponge perches on the wall's edge.

44 Hole in the Roof

This low-lying patch reef stretches from the shallows out to medium depths, offering a diverse fish population. Because of its varying depths, Hole in the Roof is a fine site for both snorkelers and divers. The primary topographic feature is a broad hole cutting through the reef. The tunnel twists and turns for more than 200ft before finally emerging onto a sand patch beneath an overhang.

Location: 1 mile (1.6km) south of Chub Cay

Depth Range: 15-50ft (4.6-15m)

Access: Boat

Expertise Rating: Novice

When you hit this sand patch, keep an eye out for garden eels and yellowhead jawfish along with flounders, conch, lizardfish and tilefish. In the rubble areas you may spot a banded jawfish. Many people overlook the marine potential of an apparently barren sand area like this one. If you keep your eyes open, however, there will be surprises.

Poised for attack, a lizardfish awaits a smaller fish for its meal.

45 Whale Point

At this site near its namesake point, sand chutes spill over the edge of the wall, gradually merging in a coral-strewn sand plain. The coral spurs here are old and have grown very tall, creating walls on either side of the sand chutes. The topography at this site is less vertical than it is at sites to the west, but it can still be considered a steep slope. The wall eventually becomes vertical, but only below accepted sport-diving limits.

There is a great deal of algal overgrowth, due to the almost complete absence of sea urchins, which are the primary algae-feeder in the islands. In the

Location: Just south of Whale Point

Depth Range: 60-130ft+ (18-40m+)

Access: Boat

Expertise Rating: Intermediate

mid-1980s the entire Caribbean region experienced a die-off of sea urchins. Though they are making a comeback, they still haven't reached a complete balance. Most of the algae is leafy and is quite attractive in its own way.

Abacos Dive Sites

Bordering the eastern rim of the Little Bahama Bank, the Abacos have an unusual air. The standard Afro-Bahamian sailing, fishing and wandering feel is supplemented by an oddly settled, stalwartly independent and very historic atmosphere. Even the local accent is a variation on the standard Bahamian, with more British influences, both in pronunciation and vocabulary. The Abacos are almost like a touch of coastal New England transplanted into the tropics.

Several of the islands in the chain are referred to as the Loyalist Cays. This dates back to the American Revolutionary War, when the Abacos saw a great influx of settlers still loyal to the British Crown from the American colonies. In reward for their British patriotism, many of the settlers were granted plots of land.

Today the influence of these early settlers is readily apparent on Green Turtle, Man O'War, Elbow and Guana Cays. The settlements are imbued with an almost impossibly perfect quaintness. The architecture is a brightly painted Victorian gingerbread style, with white picket fences and a profusion of trellis-climbing oleander, bougainvillea and hibiscus. Cars are not even permitted in the village of Hope Town on Elbow Cay, which is home to The Bahamas' most famous landmark—its candy-striped lighthouse.

Marsh Harbour, the Abacos' largest town, has a unique distinction—it's home to the one and only streetlight in the Out Islands. It is also the center of boating in the northern Bahamas. The large number of American expatriates living on the island has shifted the atmosphere from solidly Bahamian to a Florida-cum-Bahamas mix.

Though part of the Abacos, Walker's Cay demands separate consideration. This tiny cay sits a good distance from the bulk of the islands, way at the top of The Bahamas. It is a private island with one marina, one resort and a single-minded devotion to ocean sports. This is a walking island—it's barely three-quarters of a mile long, and the only motorized vehicles are a couple of utility trucks. A big fishing destination, Walker's Cay claims more IGFA

The Abacos' candy-striped lighthouse.

(International Game Fishing Association) records than any other island and hosts the world's largest private billfish tournament.

Most of the Abaco reefs are relatively shallow, though some deeper areas lie off Walker's Cay. This, in conjunction with the overall quaint atmosphere and interesting topside attractions, makes the Abacos ideal for families as well as for groups of mixed divers, snorkelers and general vacationers. The reefs of the northern Abacos in particular offer a fascinating glimpse into the life cycle of the coral reef. This area has supported lush coral growth for thousands of years. Over time, fluctuations in climate and water levels have alternately encouraged and inhibited coral growth. The reefs now exhibit an ornate base structure of extinct reef overlaid by hard-coral growth.

Abacos Dive Sites

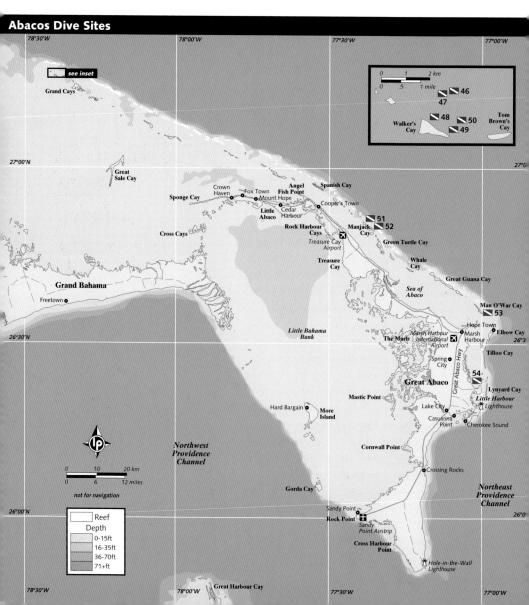

Abacos Dive Sites

	Good Snorkeling	Novice	Intermediate	Advanced
46 *Esther K & Dorothy H*			●	
47 **Shark Canyon**			●	
48 **Shark Rodeo**	●	●		
49 **Spanish Cannon & Charlie's Canyons**	●	●		
50 **Barracuda Alley**	●	●		
51 *San Jacinto*		●		
52 **Coral Caverns & Original Tarpon Dive**	●	●		
53 **Maxi Cave**	●	●		
54 **Sandy Cay**	●	●		

46 *Esther K & Dorothy H*

The *Esther K* and the *Dorothy H* are sisters, 100ft tugboats past their prime that were scuttled as artificial reefs off Walker's Cay. The intention was twofold—to add more deep dive sites and to introduce intact wrecks to the area's dive menu.

Both vessels fit the bill admirably. Each sits upright on the sand bottom in 100ft, with sparse patch reefs nearby. They were carefully prepared with diver safety in mind and thoroughly cleaned to protect the environment from pollutants.

Although these wrecks are visited as separate dives, they have many similar elements. As they were both sunk in the late 1990s, growth on the hulls is still minimal. Both vessels attract a population of barracuda, jacks and smaller fish within their hulls. Over a short time both will certainly develop coatings of sessile invertebrates and the attendant increase in fish population.

Location: Northeast of Walker's Cay

Depth Range: 78-100ft (24-30m)

Access: Boat

Expertise Rating: Intermediate

A gray angelfish glides by the *Esther K* wreck.

47 Shark Canyon

This beautiful dive features a series of long sloping canyons in the seafloor. The canyons open into a set of short tunnels created by freshwater springs flowing from small blue holes. In one place, a single tunnel that branches off into two tunnels and a short chimney, sleeping sharks are found with some regularity. These are usually Caribbean reef sharks, but divers have also seen lemon, bull and juvenile tiger sharks.

Outside the tunnels, the reef is typical of the area and is characterized by ancient spur-and-groove formations overlaid with healthy top growth and some soft

Location: Northeast of Walker's Cay

Depth Range: 65-95ft (20-29m)

Access: Boat

Expertise Rating: Intermediate

corals. The ravine also serves as a nightly gathering point for Bermuda chub. The twilight finds literally thousands of the fish settling in for the night. As the light fades, they dance and swirl in vertigo-inducing circles.

Shark Canyon is a favored resting spot for Caribbean reef sharks, as well as other shark species.

48　Shark Rodeo

One of the most thrilling shark dives in The Bahamas, Shark Rodeo easily takes the title of most attended. Conducted in a coral amphitheater over a white-sand bottom, Shark Rodeo is regularly visited by 150 to 200 sharks. The site itself is also known as **Spiral Caverns** or **Snoopy's Reef**.

Location: North of Walker's Cay

Depth: 40ft (12m)

Access: Boat

Expertise Rating: Novice

Walker's Cay is a big fishing destination and as such has an abundance of fish scraps. These scraps are frozen with water in a large barrel to form what is whimsically referred to as a chumsicle. This mass is suspended in the mid-water, between an anchor on the bottom and a buoy above. The sharks circulate, tearing pieces off the chumsicle while guests intermingle with them and observe. To acclimate yourself to the situation, you'll begin the dive as part of a group on the bottom. After a while, you can swim about as you wish, interacting with the sharks at your own personal comfort level.

While most Bahamian shark dives deal with only Caribbean reef sharks and nurse sharks, at Shark Rodeo you will encounter these plus blacktip and lemon sharks, small tiger sharks and bull sharks and the occasional hammerhead. The sharks are joined by clouds of yellowtail snappers, a dozen huge black groupers and a wide variety of other fish vying for the scraps.

Despite the large number and variety of sharks, Shark Rodeo may be the calmest and least intimidating of all Bahamian shark dives. Just be careful near the end of the dive when the melting chumsicle breaks apart—this is the only time the sharks actually get frenetic. Simply stay out of the way of the falling bait and you will be safe. Snorkelers regularly attend the Shark Rodeo, watching the action from the surface.

Sharks swarm around the "chumsicle" at Shark Rodeo.

Gary Adkison, the dive operator at Walker's Cay, has been actively tagging sharks at this site in order to track their movements through the archipelago. He collects feedback from dive opera-tors as well as from commercial and sport fishermen to get an idea of the range of tagged sharks. Some stay and some wander, but the conclusions aren't yet final.

Getting Up Close & Personal with Sharks

Few marine creatures inspire as much fear and awe as sharks. Fewer still are subject to so many myths and so much misinformation. While sharks are awe-some creatures, one of the ocean's apex predators, they are not the quite the bloodthirsty and unpredictable crea-tures they are often portrayed to be. The variety of Bahamian shark dives has contributed greatly to the general under-standing of shark behavior.

When the first Bahamian dive operator began feeding sharks some 30 years ago, it was for the macho derring-do of it all. Over the years, however, experimen-tation and experience have elevated these interactions into a safe and mea-sured dance between diver and shark.

Perhaps the most impressive trick up the shark handler's sleeve is something known as tonic immobility, which was first developed in the open ocean at the AUTEC Buoy in the Tongue of the Ocean between New Providence and Andros. Around 1990 dive operator Stuart Cove discovered that if he grabbed a silky shark by the tail and flipped it on its back while supporting its body, it would go limp for up to a minute. This trick has since been refined to the point that a handler wearing a shark suit (made from a type of chain mail commonly used in butcher's gloves) can grasp a shark by the head and stroke its snout while the animal's head rests in the handler's lap. This seems to put the shark in a sort of trance, during which the handler can actually pick up the animal (sometimes up to 7ft long!) and walk around to show the guests. After it is released, the unharmed shark simply shakes its head and swims off slowly.

How does this work? Sharks have a series of small pores on their snouts called ampul-lae of Lorenzini. These are sensory organs through which the shark "sees" its world by detecting electrical impulses. It is thought that the metal of the shark suits disrupts the shark's sensory system, putting the shark into a deep trancelike state.

For observers, however, it is important to remember that though the sharks have become accustomed to the presence of humans, they are still very much wild creatures and should be treated with appropriate caution.

49 Spanish Cannon & Charlie's Canyons

This solid mass of coral reef spreads over a big chunk of seafloor, with elkhorn corals, brain- and star-coral heads and lots of soft corals. While the fish and invertebrate life is interesting and abundant, the items that will stir your imagination are the cannon and anchors strewn across the reef, remnants of an ancient shipwreck. A damselfish has taken up residence in the barrel of the cannon, a very different load from that which the cannon once held.

At these sites (which sit close together but are dived separately) the reef itself sparks some interesting topographic variety. Undercut ledges and crevices, some accessible and some not, along with swim-throughs and other cuts create interest as well as shelter fish. The reef does not exceed 30ft and rises up to about 12ft below the surface.

Location: North side of Walker's Cay

Depth Range: 12-30ft (3.7-9.1m)

Access: Boat

Expertise Rating: Novice

A snorkeler peers into the shallow Spanish cannon.

50 Barracuda Alley

Barracuda Alley encompasses a reef and cavern system that includes several separate dive sites. Over the centuries the base structure of the reef has been eroded by weather and tidal flow into a labyrinth of interconnecting crevices and tunnels. The caverns' internal walls are coated with calcareous algaes in shades of pink and maroon. These tunnels are inhabited by clouds of baitfish surrounding reclusive groupers, jewfish and nurse sharks.

At one singularly impressive site, **Pirate's Cathedral**, a huge cavern leads

Location: ¼ mile (.4km) north of the east end Walker's Cay

Depth Range: 10-40ft (3-12m)

Access: Boat

Expertise Rating: Novice

into another, much like a massive cathedral. Shafts of light enter through chimneys in the ceiling and dance through the water, creating a beautiful, mystical feeling. The surrounding area offers an abundance of coral heads, many of them undercut into mushroom shapes.

Pirate's Cathedral is one of the area's most impressive shallow formations.

51   San Jacinto

This 234ft Civil War–era screw frigate was a square-rigged experimental vessel, one of the first ships built to test a new form of propulsion—the steam-powered engine. The *San Jacinto* slid into the water of New York Harbor in 1850, but was plagued by mechanical problems. She served honorably in blockade duty supporting Union trips and met her end in that service on the reefs of the northern Abacos on New Year's Day 1865.

The vessel now lays scattered across a sloping bottom north of Green Turtle

Location: Northeast of Green Turtle Cay

Depth Range: 35-48ft (11-15m)

Access: Boat

Expertise Rating: Novice

Cay. Her remains are covered in fire corals and various soft and hard corals. Watch for the very large green moray that makes its home here.

52   Coral Caverns & Original Tarpon Dive

The cavern formations at Coral Caverns are typical of the Abacos area. The interconnected cavern system fills seasonally with silversides, as well as an assortment of schooling southern sennets, jacks, barracuda and angelfish. A large resident grouper named Calypso will expect to be hand-fed.

Location: North of Green Turtle Cay

Depth Range: 7-50ft (2.1-15m)

Access: Boat

Expertise Rating: Novice

Feeding on the abundant smaller tropical fish, large tarpon have made the reef at Original Tarpon Dive their home. High-profile hard corals are interspersed with extinct limestone-based structures overlaid with young healthy corals, sea fans, sea plumes and other soft corals. The resident grouper ruling the roost here is known as Junkanoo.

These two dives are a few miles apart. Though they are similar and are both part of the same reef line, they must be done as individual dives.

Close encounters with friendly groupers are common.

53 Maxi Cave

This large dive site is a coral ravine that dead-ends in a coral grotto surrounded by high-profile corals. The small coral pillars are severely undercut—some look like they are nearly ready to topple under their own weight. The peaks are crowned with sea fans, sea whips, sea plumes and sea rods. Southern stingrays are commonly found in the grotto, resting undercover in the sand bottom.

Location: East of Man O'War Cay

Depth Range: 12-40ft (3.7-12m)

Access: Boat

Expertise Rating: Novice

A snorkeler admires an impeccable stand of sponges and finger corals.

54 Sandy Cay

This shallow fringing reef is one of the healthiest and most beautiful reefs in the entire country. Off the southeast shore of tiny Sandy Cay, the reef breaks the surface at the edge of the island and then slopes off nicely to 30ft. This is an ideal destination for mixed groups of snorkelers and divers.

Location: East of Sandy Cay

Depth Range: 10-33ft (3-10m)

Access: Boat

Expertise Rating: Novice

Perfect elkhorn corals dominate the shallow areas, giving way to star corals in the deeper spots. Fish abound, with peacock flounders, southern stingrays and yellow stingrays in the sand and damselfish and hamlets mingling with butterflyfish and angelfish along the reef. The reef's pristine condition is largely due to its position within the Pelican Cays Land & Sea Park.

Running north of Sandy Cay is an expansive area of sand flats called **Tiloo Bank**. Not really a dive site, it's excellent for snorkelers and makes a great sand dive for those with a discerning eye. Starfish are abundant, and dolphins come swimming through from time to time. Southern stingrays bury themselves in the sand and feed on shellfish. Photographers with sharp eyes will find bright-red juvenile scorpionfish barely an inch long, jawfish in the rubble and much more.

Tiloo Bank is an ideal place to pass a surface interval after Sandy Cay or another shallow dive, or it can make a relaxing day of exploration.

Elkhorn corals are fragile—this intact stand speaks to the untouched nature of many Bahamian reefs.

Cay Sal Dive Sites

Cay Sal Bank is accessible by live-aboard only.

Just north of Cuba, the Cay Sal Bank is visited only by cruising sailors, fishermen and divers on live-aboards from The Bahamas. Despite its proximity to the U.S.— it lies less than 50 miles (80km) from the Florida Keys—this small bank is so isolated that even cruising charts are a bit sketchy. Cay Sal Bank has only a few tiny landforms—the Anguilla Cays, the Water Cays, the Damas Cays and the Dog Rocks. The remaining rocks and shoals are barely awash at low tide.

As a dive destination, Cay Sal's intrigue comes from its isolated position. There is an abundance of blue holes and shallow reefs, as well as a lush wall on the northwest side. Big animals cruising up the Straits of Florida in the Gulf Stream add the possibility of rare and special encounters. Sharks ranging from nurses, tigers and hammerheads to the largest and most harmless shark in the sea, the whale shark, are common visitors.

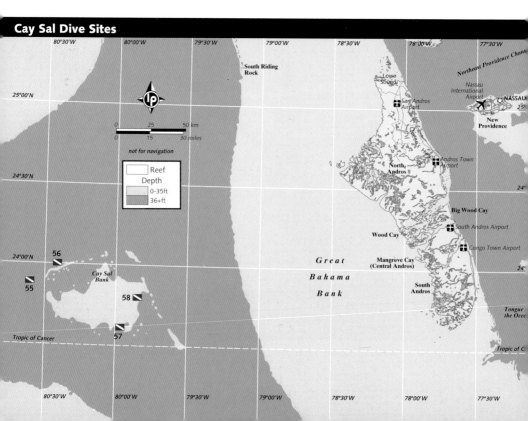

Cay Sal Dive Sites

	Good Snorkeling	Novice	Intermediate	Advanced
55 Water Cay	●	●		
56 Elbow Cay Wall			●	
57 Sistine Chapel			●	
58 Big Hole (Shark Hole)			●	

55 | Water Cay

This easy snorkel site takes you inside the limestone structure of Water Cay. Anyone with the barest free-diving skills can swim under the ledge and through the short tunnel leading to the enclosed lagoon.

Location: Inside Water Cay

Depth Range: Surface-15ft (4.6m)

Access: Live-aboard

Expertise Rating: Novice

Coral growth is minimal, but some very interesting invertebrate growth, both sessile and mobile, occupies the rough pockmarked walls of the lagoon. In the center you'll find juvenile angelfish, shifting schools of silversides, grunts and snappers, and clingfish attached to the tidal line of the limestone.

On your visit be sure to take time to wander around the island and check out its undisturbed topside nature.

Schoolmasters often drift in small to mid-sized groups.

56 Elbow Cay Wall

Elbow Cay Wall is deep, making for a relatively short dive, but the whole experience is definitely worthwhile. It is done as a drift dive, riding the flow of the Gulf Stream. Visibility is nearly always superb, easily reaching or exceeding 150ft on any given day.

Huge sponge and coral formations drip off a supremely healthy coral wall.

Location: West of Elbow Cay

Depth Range: 80-130ft+ (24-40m+)

Access: Live-aboard

Expertise Rating: Intermediate

The absolutely vertical wall plummets down from an almost square-edged peak. Big animals supplement the big growths of corals and sponges. A crewman of the dive live-aboard *Nekton Pilot* claims that every whale shark he's ever seen has been on this wall. This observation is echoed by other professionals working the area.

Look also for big jewfish, manta rays, spotted eagle rays and sharks. Elbow Cay Wall offers divers high-energy drift diving at its best.

Lush coral and sponge formations are found around every corner at Elbow Cay.

57 Sistine Chapel

One of the many blue holes found on the Cay Sal Bank, Sistine Chapel is about 125ft in diameter and has a very traditional form. It begins at 25ft, dropping more than several hundred feet in a broad bell shape. At 90ft it takes a serious cut back into the wall for nearly 100ft, creating an overhead environment.

This site's name was inspired by the massive stalactites found at around 130ft. (Stalactites are icicle-shaped calcium carbonate deposits that hang from the ceiling of caverns.) These stalactites could only

Location: 3 miles (4.8km) southwest of Damas Rocks

Depth Range: 25-130ft+ (7.6-40m+)

Access: Live-aboard

Expertise Rating: Intermediate

have formed over centuries when the cavern was exposed to air. Now flooded, it offers a great view into the geologic past.

58 Big Hole (Shark Hole)

Big Hole is a classic blue hole nearly a quarter-mile wide. This blue hole is perfect and simple—its solid lip sits in 30ft and drops down to a ledge at 50ft before plunging another 400ft straight into the unknown.

Over the years a shark dive has been carefully cultivated in this area. It has developed into a thrilling encounter. For some reason the sharks at this site are a little more nervous and active than on many Bahamian shark dives—after the bait is secured, the sharks come rising out of the depths and are simply not polite. As at other sites in The Bahamas, the males are more aggressive than the females. This dive usually attracts males. A single site will almost always attract one or the other—unless mating, they seldom mix.

The site has one mooring for live-aboards. To get to the site of the shark dive, you drop off the dive platform and swim across the deep dark hole. It can be slightly unnerving. Consider this the price you pay for admission, or just consider it an unusual thrill.

Location: West of Damas Rocks

Depth Range: 30-130ft+ (9.1-40m+)

Access: Live-aboard

Expertise Rating: Intermediate

Andros Dive Sites

The largest island in The Bahamas, Andros boasts the world's third-longest barrier reef, stretching 140 miles (225km) along the island's eastern shore. Only Belize and Australia have longer reefs. This reef defines the western edge of the Tongue of the Ocean, one of the area's most impressive deep trenches.

Andros offers some of the country's most expansive and undisturbed natural surroundings. Though large, Andros is sparsely settled, with a population of fewer than 10,000 people. Residents survive largely on fishing, farming and, to a lesser degree, tourism. Much of the island is covered with forest, home to ill-tempered wild boars and more than 40 species of wild orchids. The island's dozens of bird species make bird-watching an important attraction.

The island is divided into three large sections—actually islands themselves—separated by large sounds and further fragmented by tiny creeks. Andros is the only island in the archipelago with this formation. It has an abundant supply of fresh water, much of which is shipped daily to other islands—more than 3 million gallons (11 million liters) a day go to Nassau alone. The western backcountry is a sprawling area of mangroves and mudflats. Bonefishing is superb through the flats and the sounds.

With at least 178 inland blue holes and more than 50 oceanic blue holes, Andros has more blue holes than any island in The Bahamas, perhaps more than any area of its size in the world. Adventurers come from around the world to plumb the secrets of these blue holes.

Andros' lush, green, forested landscape differs greatly from the other islands in the archipelago.

Andros is home to Small Hope Bay, the very first offshore dive operation in The Bahamas. The late Dick Birch founded it in 1960 and was personally responsible for the early underwater exploration of the island. Some of the world's greatest underwater photographers, cave explorers and marine scientists have made this their base of operations. For the adventurous diver, Small Hope Bay offers a complete roster of specialty dives, a few of which are detailed in these pages.

For the casual sport diver, there is more to Androsian diving than just the blue holes. The barrier reef provides a wealth of shallow reefs leading to the drop-off into the Tongue. Most of the walls tend to be sloping, but there are vertical areas as well. Andros (along with San Salvador) was one of the very first places where the art of wall diving was refined. Numerous shallow coral areas inside the barrier reef are suitable for both snorkeling and diving, and a few wrecks along the coast are worth exploring.

Androsian Legends

Things that go bump in the night, the monster under the bed, the thing in the closet—we all grow up with our demons and myths, and it's certainly no different in The Bahamas. Andros' mysterious blue holes—apparently bottomless abysses that boil and suck water and seem to lead into the underworld—lend themselves perfectly to the creation of myths. The Lusca, a malevolent, dragonlike creature, is said to inhabit the blue holes. Bahamian children are warned not to swim in blue holes—the Lusca lurks in the shadows, they are told, waiting to grasp the ankle of a disobedient child and pull him beneath the surface, never to be seen again. It is clear that the myth of the Lusca was inspired by the hydrodynamics of blue holes, which boil on a dropping tide and suck water into the depths on a rising tide. The Lusca serves as an apt safety warning.

On mythology's gentler side, it is also believed that mermaids inhabit the holes. Shy and retiring, they avoid contact with people and are rarely seen. To catch a glimpse of one of these nymphs, you must approach the blue hole very quietly. At the slightest sound, the mermaids dive into the hole, leaving only a surface ripple as evidence of their existence.

Another mythical Androsian creature is the Chickcharnie. These forest-dwelling little people are thought to have three toes, three fingers, red eyes and the ability to turn their heads all the way around. The creatures are fickle, with both benevolent and evil sides. The legend is used to frighten young children, as in, "If you're not good, the Chickcharnie will come in the middle of the night and steal you away." On the other hand, to sight a Chickcharnie in the vast pine forest was considered good fortune.

The basis for the Chickcharnie legend is probably animal in nature. At one time a population of 3ft- (.9m-) tall flightless owls—remote cousins of the common barn owl—inhabited the high pines of Andros. Owls are territorial in nature and no doubt gave rise to the legend of aggressive Chickcharnies dropping out of trees onto unsuspecting forest wanderers. Though extinct for more than two centuries, these owls live on in the legends of Andros.

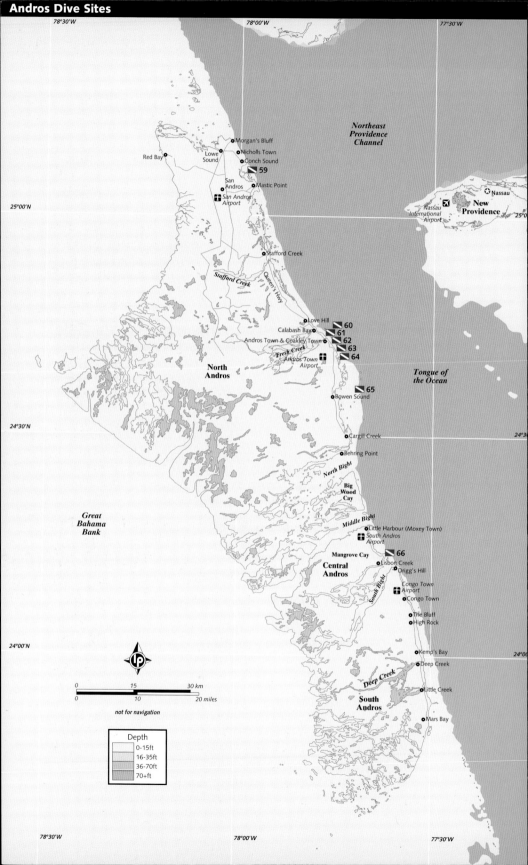

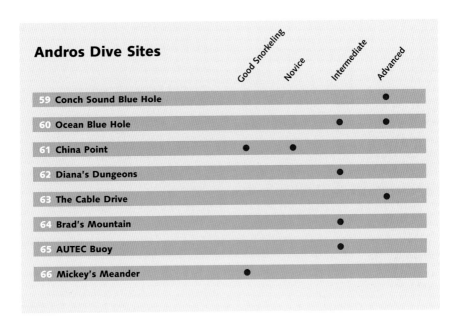

Andros Dive Sites

	Good Snorkeling	Novice	Intermediate	Advanced
59 Conch Sound Blue Hole				●
60 Ocean Blue Hole			●	●
61 China Point		●	●	
62 Diana's Dungeons			●	
63 The Cable Drive				●
64 Brad's Mountain			●	
65 AUTEC Buoy			●	
66 Mickey's Meander	●			

59 Conch Sound Blue Hole

Though it seems simple at first, Conch Sound Blue Hole is a specialty dive, due primarily to the extremely strong flow of water during tidal exchanges. It should not be undertaken without a qualified guide and should be done only on a one-on-one basis.

The cavern begins at 10ft. You'll pass an old fishing vessel reputed to have been sucked into the opening during a strong outflow. Lots of schooling fish make this interesting even in shallow depths, but even snorkeling near the opening is strongly discouraged due to the very real danger of spiraling down-currents.

Location: Conch Sound

Depth Range: 10-90ft (3-27m)

Access: Shore

Expertise Rating: Advanced

Beyond the entrance the shaft angles down gently to 90ft and evens off into a horizontal passage running under the island for more than 3,500ft. Sponges, sparse corals, crabs and lobsters cling to the walls, offering marine-life interest.

60 Ocean Blue Hole

This impressive blue hole is very different in form than the normal Bahamian blue hole. It is actually a cave opening in the side of the Andros wall, a place where a past cataclysmic event caused the wall to collapse into a massive cavern system. The primary external feature is an elongated horizontal oval with two separate openings. The dive plan varies according to the diver's expertise. Ocean Blue Hole was initially explored by the folks at Small Hope Bay, who defined it as a three-tiered cavern/cave dive. Level I is on the standard dive list, while Levels II and III are considered specialty dives because of their depths and the complicated cavern system.

Level I is a simple swim through the shallowest portion of the system. Divers enter at the north opening at about 40ft, proceed through the cavern and emerge at the southern opening. You will explore the back of the initial cavern and discover a freshwater river, the flow issuing from an inland spring. Be cautious—it's easy to drop below your planned depth, as the cavern floor lies below sport-diving levels. Level I divers should not go below 100ft.

Location: Northeast of Fresh Creek

Depth Range: 40-130ft+ (12-40m+)

Access: Boat

Expertise Rating: Intermediate to Advanced

Level II—only for the very advanced diver—goes into a large tunnel with the ceiling at 140ft and the floor at 320ft. Divers proceed just under the ceiling and emerge into an area where shafts of light shine through a broken ceiling above. From there you proceed into one of the largest underwater caverns in The Bahamas before exiting the system.

The basic profile of Level III is for the highly trained specialty diver only. You enter by following a fault line into the wall to a depth of 190ft. Even at that depth, you're still well above the system's maximum depth and well out of the breadth of the system. Exploration beyond the basic profile can only be undertaken by professional underwater cave explorers.

Ocean Blue Hole is the most famous of Andros' many oceanic and inland blue holes.

61 China Point

China Point is just one of many shallow reefs sheltered inside Andros' barrier reef and wall. It features some of the nicest freestanding corals in the area, with large formations of elkhorn, star and brain corals scattered across a shallow sandy seafloor.

Location: Near Fresh Creek

Depth Range: 10-15ft (3-4.6m)

Access: Boat

Expertise Rating: Novice

The first thing you'll notice at the site are schools of sergeant majors, along with squirrelfish, triggerfish, Nassau groupers, trumpetfish, angelfish and a host of invertebrates on the corals themselves.

Nearby **Red Shoal** is a lone, almost-circular patch of elkhorn corals rising from the bottom to within feet of the surface. Large schools of French and striped grunts take shelter under the coral, along with many other tropicals. Also of note in this area are **Central Point, Liben's Point** and **Trumpet Reef.** All are in the same depth range and offer excellent snorkeling and great opportunities for fish-watching and photography. While on-island, ask about snorkeling from shore.

Snorkelers can explore many shallow reefs off Andros' shores.

62 Diana's Dungeons

This site is representative of the hundreds of wall sites east of the Andros' barrier reef. It is named for the many caverns and chimneys it encompasses. Large openings are penetrated by shafts of sunlight shining through breaks in the reef. Silversides fill the caverns, parting like curtains at a diver's approach.

The site sits on the edge of the wall, so divers have a choice of exploring the caverns or dropping over the edge into the abyss. Look for eagle rays, sharks and turtles. The maximum depth in the caverns is 90ft, while over the wall you'll encounter depths well beyond sport-diving limits.

Location: Just east of Small Hope Bay

Depth Range: 70-130ft+ (21-40m+)

Access: Boat

Expertise Rating: Intermediate

While you're thinking about Andros wall diving, consider inquiring about the following sites: **Hanging Gardens Wall, Nitrox Express, Giant's Staircase, Turnbull's Gut** and **Len's Lost Wall**. All are tremendous. In addition, some of the best sites are those without names.

Though sea turtle populations are threatened worldwide, you may see them at Diana's Dungeons.

Deep Diving

Over the past decade, deep diving—that is, diving below the accepted sport-diving limit of 130ft (40m)—has become a reality in a variety of destinations throughout the world, including The Bahamas. Specific certifying agencies have dedicated themselves to training divers in the safe exploration of environments formerly considered inaccessible to sport divers.

Two main certifying agencies—IANDT and TDI—specialize in what is often called technical (or tech) diving. With the advances made in deep diving, technical diving pros from around the world have explored many of the blue holes and deep waters of The Bahamas. At this point, the islands best suited to technical disciplines are Andros, New Providence and Grand Bahama, but new possibilities crop up regularly in other areas of the country as well.

Divers in The Bahamas have established world records in deep diving and deep cave penetration, thanks to a combination of the country's tech-diving potential and the divers' personal bravado. If your intent is to explore the barely known, you must understand the degree of training necessary to undertake this safely. Do not even consider attempting these endeavors solo. Instead, look for facilities offering technical diver training.

63　The Cable Dive

This unusual dive takes advantage of a cable anchored on the seafloor of the Tongue of the Ocean in 6000ft. Used to pull objects down to depth and measure their ascent speed under varying pressure differentials, the cable also provides an orienting focus for this deep-blue ocean experience.

On land the cable is anchored to the AUTEC Ocean Haul-Down Tower. Underwater it goes through an anchored loop at 50ft, passes over the wall and finally plunges down into the blue. The attraction of this site is the same as at any deep blue dive—the chance to view stupendous pelagics, from billfish or

Location: East of Andros Town

Depth Range: Surface-130ft+ (40m+)

Access: Boat or shore

Expertise Rating: Advanced

sharks, to chains of transparent pelagic tunicates, to a wealth of other potential encounters.

The dive begins where the cable enters the water. Divers descend hand over hand down the line until they reach a turn-around point because of one of three limiting factors—10 minutes, the one-third air rule (first diver to exhaust a third of his or her air) or a maximum of 200ft. At that point, divers begin their return, approaching and ascending the vertical wall. The dive is concluded with a decompression stop surrounded by schooling fish at 20ft under the tower. The Cable Dive is a specialty dive, done only with a very tight divemaster-to-diver ratio.

Atlantic spadefish are named for their distinct shape, which resembles a spade on a playing card.

64 Brad's Mountain

A coral structure sitting within the barrier reef, Brad's Mountain is a perfect medium-depth dive. The site's focus is a coral mountain that rises from the sand at about 50ft to a peak about 15ft below the surface.

This very healthy reef mound features lush invertebrate growth, along with many tropicals and schooling fish. Expect to encounter schools of Atlantic spadefish and Bermuda chub, as well as a variety of grunts and jacks.

Location: South of Fresh Creek

Depth Range: 15-50ft (4.6-15m)

Access: Boat

Expertise Rating: Intermediate

The interior is honeycombed with tunnels and small caverns, which are often populated by shimmering groups of silversides. Watch for moray eels entwined in the reef.

65 AUTEC Buoy

This dive provides an extraordinary blue-water experience. The AUTEC Buoy is a naval buoy anchored in 6,000ft that is used mainly for submarine training exercises and experiments by the U.S. Navy. The buoy is huge—a barrel some 15ft in diameter. Below this massive float hangs a chain composed of huge links attached to a very long cable. This site is accessed from both Andros as well as New Providence on a regular basis.

The attraction? Blue-water pelagics are drawn to the humming sound the cable makes as it is strummed by deep currents flowing through the Tongue of the Ocean. Beneath the buoy you'll find schools of jacks, silky sharks, dolphin-fish and many other denizens of the deep.

Location: Tongue of the Ocean, east of central Andros

Depth Range: Surface-130ft+ (40m+)

Access: Boat

Expertise Rating: Intermediate

Keep a close eye on your depth gauge during this dive! The experience of dropping into this pelagic community of the deep has a surprising effect. It is amazing how similar 20ft seems to 100ft and how easy it is to reach a depth greater than planned. Also keep an eye on the endless blue surrounding you. You never know what lurks at the edge of visibility.

Divers use a line to descend from the dive boat into the depths.

66 Mickey's Meander

Viable sites in Andros' southern region tend to be shallow or intermediate reefs, as the wall begins deeper here than in the north reaches of the barrier reef. The diving off the southeast coast of Andros is relatively virgin, while the Out Island atmosphere of the place makes it further worthy of a special stop. Mickey's Meander is a good example of the offerings available in this area.

You roll off the side of the boat and drop to a sand bottom at 45ft. From there proceed along a horseshoe-shaped reef for about 200 yards. A 30ft-long cavern leads into a hallway with coral walls on each side. Return back along the reef to a huge coral head called Christmas Tree, which rises to 22ft. You can enjoy the prolific fish life as you off-gas.

Location: Off Mangrove Cay

Depth Range: 46-58ft (14-18m)

Access: Boat

Expertise Rating: Novice

Marine life along the way includes eagle rays, a few sharks and other pelagics (some predatory) and lots of curious tropicals.

A fine nearby site is **Grouper Canyon**. A series of swim-throughs and shallow chutes lead through a reef, with depths ranging from about 22 to 52ft. Schools of Bermuda chub and horse-eye jacks predominate in the mid-water, while tropicals swarm around nurse sharks resting on the bottom.

A dusky damselfish jealously guards its patch of eggs from predators.

Eleuthera Dive Sites

The northeast corner of the Great Bahama Bank is bordered by the island of Eleuthera (from *eleutheria*, the Greek word for freedom). Just 40 miles (64km) east of New Providence, the island is shaped like a sickle. It's more than 100 miles (161km) long, but only 1 to 3 miles (1.6 to 4.8km) wide for most of its length.

Eleuthera was colonized in 1649 by the Eleutherian Adventurers, a group of several dozen religious dissidents—Puritans, in this case—from British-controlled Bermuda. These early settlers came upon Eleuthera in the worst possible fashion—they were shipwrecked on the Devil's Backbone, a ragged shallow reef that borders the north end of the island less than a half-mile (.8km) offshore. Stranded, they decided that fate had spoken and they settled on the island, forming the New World's first republic.

On its north end Eleuthera is flanked by many small cays and two significant islands—Spanish Wells and Harbour Island, both of which are reachable by water taxi only. The center of Bahamian lobstering, Spanish Wells is probably the wealthiest community of local residents in The Bahamas. Harbour Island, off Eleuthera's northeast tip, is one of the country's prettiest communities. Famed for pink beaches—the result of conch shells turned to sand—Harbour Island is a great getaway vacation spot. Known locally by the shortened name "Briland," the island is small enough to explore on foot and interesting enough to make the stroll worthwhile. The main street through Dunmore Town is lined with historic gingerbreaded homes. Harbour Island is reached by water taxi from the mainland after flying into the airport on the north end of Eleuthera (there are three airports on Eleuthera).

Many ships have met their fates on the treacherous Devil's Backbone reef.

Virtually every rocky point in the entire area gives way to coral- and sponge-encrusted boulders lying in the sand. Many of these are accessible from shore. Although the waters around Eleuthera's south end offer some fine walls, there are no professional dive operations in that area, with the exception of a Club Med. Most diving takes place in the north, out of Harbour Island, which is home to two very good professional dive operators. There are sites along shallow and deep reefs on the Atlantic side, as well as on the expansive shallow reefs along the Devil's Backbone, to the north. This treacherous, jagged reef has claimed many ships over the years. The combination of shallow reefs, wrecks and abundant marine life makes for a fascinating diving experience.

Eleuthera Dive Sites

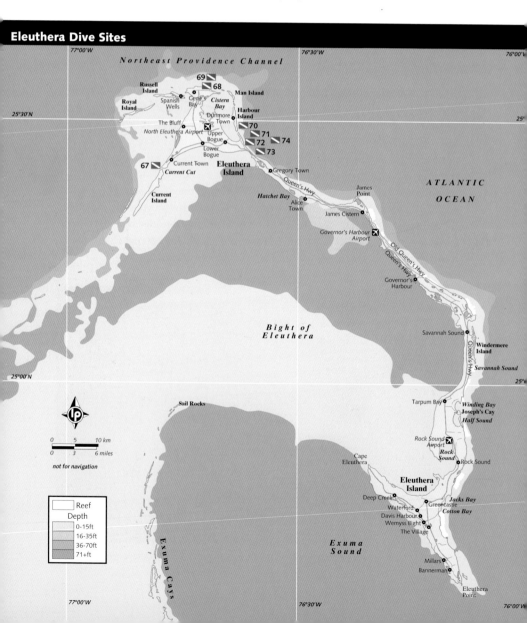

Eleuthera Dive Sites

	Good Snorkeling	Novice	Intermediate	Advanced
67 Current Cut			●	
68 Bat Cave & Bone Sink Hole				●
69 Devil's Backbone Wrecks	●	●		
70 Pink House Reef	●	●		
71 The Arch			●	
72 The Plateau		●		
73 Glass Window Bridge			●	
74 The Pinnacle				●

67 Current Cut

Current Cut lies in the narrow channel between the western tip of North Eleuthera and Current Island. Only about 100 yards wide at the most, the channel acts like the neck of a funnel during the tidal exchange, producing currents of up to 7 to 9 knots (8.4 to 11mph).

The channel can be dived on either a rising or falling tide. You approach from outside the channel and wait for the current to pick you up for the Superman flight of all time. You can escape the current momentarily by ducking behind structures or into potholes in the limestone bottom. The trip lasts less than 10 minutes, before the current spits you out the opposite side. Most divers will go through several times on a single visit.

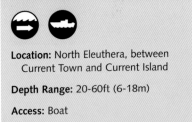

Location: North Eleuthera, between Current Town and Current Island

Depth Range: 20-60ft (6-18m)

Access: Boat

Expertise Rating: Intermediate

As you scream through the often-murky water, you'll pass sharks, turtles and eagle rays. Swimming into the current, the animals appear to be suspended motionless, feeding on whatever chance may bring. On occasion it's possible to see more than three dozen spotted eagle rays on a single pass.

68 Bat Cave & Bone Sink Hole

These two inland blue holes are suited for advanced divers with cavern/cave certification only. The two holes are close to one another and are most likely interconnected, though that has not yet been conclusively determined.

Both are typical blue holes, dropping down somewhat vertically and then

Location: Inland near Preacher's Cave on Eleuthera's north end

Depth Range: Surface-100ft (30m)

Access: Land

Expertise Rating: Advanced

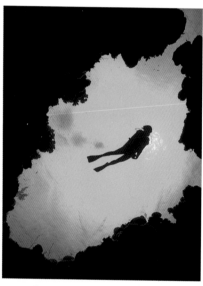

Exploring Eleuthera's inland blue holes.

belling out. Visibility is very good year-round in both holes. Both dives should be treated as cavern dives at the very least. Unless you are well trained in cave diving, be sure to always keep within sight of the light issuing from the opening.

The caves are still being explored by the folks at Valentine's Dive Center, and much remains to be accomplished in terms of discovery as well as the logistics of laying lines and mapping the systems. At present Bat Cave does have some line laid out. Bone Sink Hole requires some physical exertion to enter and exit, as the opening is about 40ft below ground level. You must plan ahead and come prepared.

69 Devil's Backbone Wrecks

The *Cienfuegos*, a 292ft American steamship, operated as a passenger liner. On February 5, 1895, the ship was passing through the Northeast Providence Channel in a strong northwest gale, when she ran aground on the ragged peaks of the Devil's Backbone.

Irretrievably snagged, she was doomed. Thanks to the skill and bravery of the native Eleutherians, every passenger and crewmember was saved. The *Cienfuegos* is now thoroughly flattened, but her bow,

Location: Devil's Backbone, north of Eleuthera

Depth Range: 8-35ft (2.4-11m)

Access: Boat

Expertise Rating: Novice

steam engines and boilers are still recognizable under a coating of marine life.

A diver visits the encrusted anchor of a ship wrecked on the Devil's Backbone reef.

The **Potato & Onion Wreck**, named for its original cargo, is actually the remains of the *Vanaheim*. In February 1969, the 86ft coastal freighter rammed into the Devil's Backbone, ending up nearly on top of the *Cienfuegos*.

About 100 yards west of these wrecks lies the **Train Wreck**, a Civil War–era Union train that was captured by the Confederacy and sold to a Cuban sugar plantation. It was lost during a storm in 1865, when the wooden barge carrying her foundered. Look for the huge wheels sitting in just 15ft.

Resting just 100 yards east of the *Cienfuegos*, the **Carnarvon** met her end in 1916. A 186ft Welsh freighter, she sits dismembered on a sand bottom in only

35ft. Her anchors, boilers, engines and huge propeller make for excellent photo ops. As with the other wrecks in the area, the vessel's proximity to the surface and shallow reeftop make the site great for snorkelers also.

Since the structure of the Devil's Backbone is very consistent, all of these wrecks share a very similar topography and variety of marine life. The coral heads reach nearly to the surface, with some of the shallowest reefs inside the Backbone nearly awash at low tide. The exposure to open-ocean conditions is punishing, a fact that is evident in the amount of extinct coral on the reefs. The structures themselves are very interesting—you'll find high-profile corals with undercuts and angular, jagged edges.

Fish life here is typical of The Bahamas, with the usual cast of characters—angelfish, parrotfish, grunts, snappers and an abundance of small tropicals. You're also likely to find some lobsters, crabs and moray eels.

A wheel from the Civil War–era Train Wreck.

70 Pink House Reef

Pink House Reef is one of the most popular snorkeling reefs off Harbour Island. It has plenty of smaller life to keep macrophotographers busy. Sea slugs, tunicate clusters and cup corals combine with shrimp, anemones and tropicals to keep the shutter clicking.

The many small tunnels running through the reef fill seasonally with silversides—summer is peak time. When silversides are present, you'll also find tarpon and jacks preying on this abundant food source. The site's varied

Location: .5 miles (.8km) north of Harbour Mouth

Depth Range: 5-20ft (1.5-6m)

Access: Boat

Expertise Rating: Novice

topography offers shelter to large and small fish, so keep a sharp eye on the holes in the reef to see what you can find.

71　The Arch

One of the island's better deep sites lies directly east of Harbour Mouth, the opening at the southern end of Harbour Island. The Arch is a 50ft-long tunnel that cuts through the spurs. Though its bottom reaches 114ft, the majority of the dive usually happens between 65 and 85ft. Sea fans and black corals frame the arch itself, and the entire area features excellent invertebrate growth.

This is the southern end of Miller's Reef, a reef system bordering the entire Atlantic (eastern) side of Harbour Island. The reef exhibits a classic high-profile spur-and-groove formation. Exposure to the Atlantic Ocean guarantees good pelagic and reef fish life but also presents occasionally challenging water conditions. The boat ride, as well as the entry and exit from the craft, can be difficult, so be certain your experience level is up to it.

Location: Just east of Harbour Mouth

Depth Range: 65-114ft (20-35m)

Access: Boat

Expertise Rating: Intermediate

A wealth of deepwater gorgonians adorns the steep slopes off of Eleuthera.

72　The Plateau

A half-mile offshore, this large area of classically perfect spur-and-groove formations is typical of northern Eleuthera. The area is home to three distinct dive sites equipped with dive moorings—**Fish Bowl**, **The Canyons** and **The Maze**.

Location: 3 miles (4.8km) south of Harbour Mouth

Depth Range: 35-80ft (11-24m)

Access: Boat

Expertise Rating: Novice

The topography of The Canyons and The Maze is evident from their names. At The Canyon, large coral overhangs are separated by sandy grooves. Large schools of horse-eye jacks circle the heads while snappers shelter under the ledges. In The Maze, interconnecting ledges and tunnels are populated by angelfish and butterflyfish. Chromis occupy the mid-water area.

Fish Bowl is just what it sounds like—hordes of smaller tropicals like fairy basslets, gobies and wrasses mingle with schools of grunts and snappers. Look under ledges for nurse sharks and out toward the open water for eagle rays.

The fairy basslet is one of the most strikingly colorful inhabitants of Bahamian reefs.

73 Glass Window Bridge

This site sits immediately off (and is named for) the bridge connecting the thin spit of northern Eleuthera with central Eleuthera. Until the 1980s a rock bridge high above the channel connected the two portions of the island. The spot is named for this rock bridge, which from the sea looked like a massive glass window. The bridge, battered by ocean tides during an annual local phenomenon called The Rage, eventually collapsed. The Rage is a period of high winds and high tides that sends crashing waves, whose spray reaches as much as 150ft above the tall cliffs.

This is a great dive with tons of life. The dive site is a scattered plain of boul-

Location: East of Glass Window Bridge

Depth Range: 25-61ft (7.6-19m)

Access: Boat

Expertise Rating: Intermediate

ders dislodged over the years from the cliffs above. Tumbled together, they now form caverns and small tunnels occupied by Nassau groupers, tarpon, jacks and snappers. Hard-coral growth is minimal, but you'll see plenty of encrusting sponges and coralline algae. Beware of boat traffic in the area.

74 The Pinnacle

Sitting about 3 miles offshore, The Pinnacle is a spectacular open-ocean dive featuring blue-water pelagics. Here big sharks, sport fish such as amberjacks and wahoo, and large schools of jacks and snappers are the rule. In addition to the gamefish and pelagics, you'll also find large black coral trees and barrel sponges reaching 6 to 7ft tall.

Location: 6 miles (9.7km) southeast of Harbour Mouth

Depth Range: 99-128ft (30-39m)

Access: Boat

Expertise Rating: Advanced

The mooring is attached to the peak of the seamount at 99ft, near a good-sized archway that cuts through the pinnacle. The reef takes many forms as it rolls across the open-ocean plateau. There are sloping walls, as well as areas where the reef drops into canyons before rising up again.

The Pinnacle is surrounded by deep waters, but they aren't part of the normal dive plan. The seamount itself is rather deep, so time is limited, and most divers seldom venture from the mooring. The site's depth and currents mean it is only for divers able to handle the conditions.

Basket and barrel sponges crown rich coral formations around Eleuthera.

Exumas Dive Sites

From the air, the islands of the Exuma chain present that irresistible and unmistakable tropical image—a necklace of pearls stretched out on a carpet of pale blue velvet. Mostly uninhabited, these islands are natural gems. The islands skirt the east edge of the Great Bahama Bank, stretching nearly 150 miles (241km). The northernmost cay, Ship Channel Cay, lies about 35 miles (56km) east of New Providence. At the chain's southern extremity, take time to cross the Tropic of Cancer—it cuts right through the center of Little Exuma.

Diving in the Exumas presents a full range of opportunities, with the focus on shallow reef systems. People like to say there are 365 islands in the chain—one for each day of the year. In reality, literally thousands of cays, islets and rocks stretch up and down the chain, and each one is home to a significant population of fascinating marine life. The cuts between the islands are exceptional due to continuous tidal flows. This constant flow of nutrients feeds the hard and soft corals, which attract abundant marine life. Sharks, rays, turtles and other larger critters visit in search of tasty morsels that float in on the current.

Accessible walls to the north are truly superb—vertical and undercut with huge sponges and black coral trees. The Exumas also boast a number of fascinating blue holes. The diver-friendly blue holes are clustered around Great Exuma and

The rare Exuma iguana is found only on Allan's Cay.

126

its surrounding cays and islets. As always, you should not penetrate beyond view of the entrance unless you are properly trained in cave diving.

Unfortunately, exploring the Exumas can be difficult, since the majority of the islands can only be visited via live-aboard vessels or private boats. Great Exuma is home to a couple of dive operations, which offer service to the lower cays. Lodgings are small, ranging from historic properties, to simple but comfortable hotels, to downright rustic digs. Some New Providence dive operators make special trips to the northern cays, and some powerboat operators offer regular snorkeling-only trips.

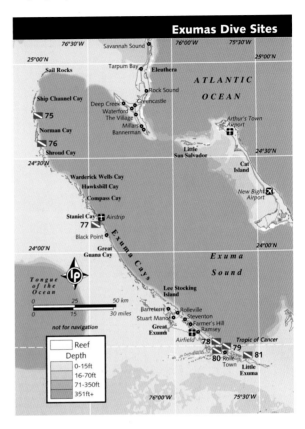

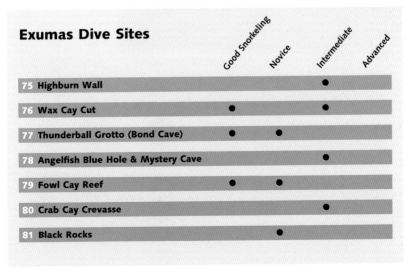

Exumas Dive Sites

	Good Snorkeling	Novice	Intermediate	Advanced
75 Highburn Wall			●	
76 Wax Cay Cut	●		●	
77 Thunderball Grotto (Bond Cave)	●	●		
78 Angelfish Blue Hole & Mystery Cave			●	
79 Fowl Cay Reef	●	●		
80 Crab Cay Crevasse			●	
81 Black Rocks		●		

75 Highburn Wall

Highburn Wall is both the name of a specific dive area as well as the generic name for the extensive drop-off that stretches miles down the Exuma Cays. Because the area is a long way from any land-based operation, it is seldom dived except by live-aboard dive vessels.

Location: East of Highburn Cay

Depth Range: 50-130ft+ (15-40m+)

Access: Boat

Expertise Rating: Intermediate

This exceedingly unusual octocoral is found off Great Exuma.

Individual site names along the drop-off vary, and none have become an important part of the dive menu. The wall is typified by a steep slope to a 110ft shelf, where it levels off before another steep drop into Exuma Sound.

Typical marine life includes some cascading sheet corals and star corals dressed up with huge barrel and tube sponges and flanked by various types of black coral. The area's isolation also means it attracts big fish and lots of pelagics.

76 Wax Cay Cut

Wax Cay Cut is one of the prettiest shallow cuts in the Exumas and is highly regarded. An extensive and extremely healthy coral reef stretches out from the east and west sides of the cut. Beautiful, healthy corals stand high off the bottom. Though the site sits outside of the official Exuma Cays Land & Sea Park boundaries, it is isolated enough to remain virtually untouched.

Location: Between Wax Cay and Little Wax Cay

Depth Range: 7-46ft (2.1-14m)

Access: Boat

Expertise Rating: Intermediate

The current flows between 1 to 3 knots (1.2 to 3.5 miles/hr) on an incoming or outgoing tide, so Wax Cay Cut is usually done as a drift dive during the tidal exchange. Expect to see lots of groupers and a flurry of other fish life. Look also for lobster antennae poking out of holes in the reef. Sharks pass through here, often hanging in the current as the tides change. It's also possible to see turtles and multitudes of schooling fish. You'll want to do multiple drops at this site.

Snorkelers explore another of the many perfectly formed coral heads in the Exumas.

77 Thunderball Grotto (Bond Cave)

The pristine location and variety of forms along this reef have made it an ideal background for several films, most notably the James Bond film *Thunderball*. The actual cave is inside a small island on the west side of Staniel Cay.

At 110ft long and 80ft across, the giant hollow dome occupies nearly two-thirds of the interior of the island. Half the cave is above the waterline. Lots of light filters through the perforated ceiling, speckling the interior with dancing rays. The walls inside the cave are lined with white crinoids, encrusting sponges, coralline algae and an assortment of small corals.

Location: Off Staniel Cay

Depth Range: 5-30ft (1.5-9.1m)

Access: Boat

Expertise Rating: Novice

Outside the cave you'll find a striking section of reef that features small and healthy individual coral heads scattered across the sand bottom. Southern stingrays feed in the sand, keeping company with jacks, angelfish, mojarras and other small sand-flat dwellers.

78 Angelfish Blue Hole & Mystery Cave

The Angelfish Blue Hole is an oceanic blue hole close to Georgetown on Great Exuma. Stocking Island is one

Location: Stocking Island

Depth Range: 25-90ft (7.6-27m)

Access: Boat

Expertise Rating: Intermediate

Angelfish Blue Hole's semi-tame mascot.

of the islands forming the eastern barrier of Elizabeth Harbour. It has a small bay that doglegs back into the island. The bay is a classic hurricane hole—that is, a protected bay used by yachts during severe storms. Near this lagoon's back end you'll find the blue hole's 30ft-wide opening in about 25ft of water. This classic circular entryway leads into a cavern that drops to 90ft and then runs back about 400ft to an apparent dead end.

Named for the semi-tame angelfish that greet divers approaching the cavern, Angelfish Blue Hole is a perfect introduction to blue-hole diving. The opening remains visible throughout the entire dive. Schools of grunts and clusters of lobsters inhabit the interior, while divers often see eagle rays on the outside. For clear conditions, dive it on a slack low tide.

Mystery Cave sits just across the lagoon, only 20 yards from Angelfish Blue Hole. A narrow elliptical opening shelters snappers and grunts and leads to a complex system of caverns.

Tight and silty, Mystery Cave is for experienced cave divers only. Though the initial room is large—40ft in diameter—

the tunnels quickly narrow and are only partially accessible to explorers. The cave slants down at a 30-degree angle to about 60ft before flattening out and running east beneath Stocking Island to the ocean.

The system was explored and mapped by Jacques Cousteau and his team in the mid-1960s. They penetrated the system for 1,800ft but were unable to complete the passage. Dye released in the hole on an outgoing current has been sighted 2 miles offshore, confirming a connection to several other local oceanic blue holes. Efforts to complete this system have never been finished.

79   Fowl Cay Reef

This pretty reef butts up against both Guana Cay and Fowl Cay, sloping into the sand plain separating them. It's a typically calm Exuma reef, with healthy corals and lots of little things to maintain interest.

Fowl Cay Reef is a very small reef—it is simply the underwater growth that creeps off the edge of a tiny island before dropping into a narrow channel between this cay and the next pearl in the chain. Despite its diminutive proportions, it is a gem. You aren't likely to find large fish, but if you're interested in the small things that keep a reef alive, you'll love this dive. If you prefer to cover a quarter-mile on every dive, you'll have to look else-where. Fowl Cay Reef is for people who can sit and watch.

The north end of **Guana Cay** (south of Elisabeth Cay) offers a similar reef, with a little more depth and even higher-profile coral heads. Look for stingrays and flounders resting in the sand.

Location: Between Guana and Fowl Cays

Depth Range: 6-20ft (1.8-6m)

Access: Boat

Expertise Rating: Novice

Shallow heads attract fish on Fowl Cay Reef.

The Exuma Cays Land & Sea Park

The Exuma Cays Land & Sea Park is The Bahamas' largest marine reserve and is an admirable effort toward preserving a pristine area. Established in 1956 and administered by the Bahamas National Trust, the park encompasses 176 sq miles (456 sq km) of island and ocean bottom in the northern reaches of the Exuma Cays.

This small chunk of sand and water epitomizes the natural beauty of The Bahamas. Beginning at Wax Cay Cut on the north end and reaching south to Conch Cut, the park extends 22 miles (35km) from northwest to southeast and is about 8 miles (13km) wide. Within these boundaries lie eight primary cays and dozens of tiny islets and exposed rocks. The cuts between the cays are alive with marine life, the result of the constant flow of water, which creates a perfect feeding ground. Divers will find sharks and rays, groupers and snappers, crabs and lobsters and a seemingly endless kaleidoscopic array of marine life.

The park is an absolute no-take zone for marine and plant life, alive or dead, including dead shellfish. Lobstering and fishing, whether by line or spear, are prohibited. Pollution or littering in any form is also forbidden. These uninhabited islands offer a wealth of natural attractions, and the Bahamian government intends to keep it that way.

On land, bird-watching visitors can observe numerous species, including seabirds such as terns, waders or tropicbirds. Iguanas and curly-tailed lizards scamper across the sand. Turtles swim in the shallows and nest on the beaches. On Hawksbill Cay, marked nature trails lead to the ruins of a Loyalist plantation. Warderick Wells Cay sports another 4 miles (6.4km) of marked nature trails. On Shroud Cay visit Driftwood Village, a collection of folk art constructed of flotsam and jetsam washed up on the shores of the islands. You may also want to visit the cave on the Rocky Dundas in the Conch Cay Cut.

80 Crab Cay Crevasse

This is a very accessible blue hole with an oblong opening leading into an extensive cavern and cave system. Three separate tunnels lead into the system, and there is plenty of fish life near the opening, adding to the aura surrounding the blue hole. This extensive cavern has quite a reach to it. In some areas the ceiling still sports eroded remnants of stalactites formed long ago when sea levels were lower.

Location: In the channel west of Crab Cay

Depth Range: 20-120ft (6-37m)

Access: Boat

Expertise Rating: Intermediate

You can do quite a bit of exploring while still maintaining a line of sight with the opening, but exercise caution. It's easy to penetrate farther than you intend, as the main rooms are large and thus deceptively safe. Always remember that it's easy to get turned around, a sure recipe for disaster for the untrained or ill-equipped diver. Don't venture beyond sight of light from the opening without proper training and a solid plan. At the end of the dive you may want to spend time exploring the sand flats outside the opening to see what kind of sand dwellers you scare up.

A diver explores a tunnel at Crab Cay Crevasse.

81 Black Rocks

Location: North of Little Exuma

Depth Range: 50-70ft (15-21m)

Access: Boat

Expertise Rating: Novice

Black Rocks covers a fairly large area between Great and Little Exuma and is popular with visiting yachties as well as dedicated traveling divers. Isolated coral heads, all fairly large and with 10 to 15ft of relief, are strewn about the seafloor. The heads are largely made of dead coral but do feature some excellent sponge growth and superficial hard-coral surface growth. Despite the limited live coral growth, you can expect to see stingrays, parrotfish and some conchs feeding in the sand. If you search carefully, you may also see banded jawfish excavating their burrows in the rubble areas.

Cat Island Dive Sites

Bonefish quietly feeding in the mud, ruins of long-abandoned plantations, land crabs large enough to scare you, monarch moths the size of bats, traditions of Obeah (Afro-Caribbean sorcery and magic ritual) mixed with bush medicine, older islanders who consider a trip of 40 miles (64km) to be a major journey—Cat Island provides many good examples of the heart of Bahamian life. The island is boot-shaped, 48 miles (77km) long and seldom more than a few miles wide. Of the Bahamian islands that offer professional dive services, Cat Island is one of the least visited and most genuinely Bahamian.

The origin of the island's name is uncertain, but it may be connected to Arthur Catt, an infamous pirate who used the island as his base of operations. The island

A snorkeler visits an offshore islet.

is a combination of densely forested acres juxtaposed with swamp and mangrove areas. Bonefishing is considered excellent in the creek openings. Caves, blue holes and freshwater lakes dot the island.

Points of interest include Mount Alvernia—at 206ft (63m), it is the highest point in The Bahamas. It is also the location of the Hermitage, a refuge built by Father Jerome, an Anglican priest who lived on Cat Island. When the priest

Cat Island Dive Sites	Good Snorkeling	Novice	Intermediate	Advanced
82 Dry Heads	●	●		
83 Greenwood Reef	●	●		
84 Black Coral Wall			●	
85 The Cut	●	●		
86 Devil's Point				●
87 Tartar Bank				●

passed away in 1956, he was interred on the stone slab he used for a bed in the cave he called home. His memory is treasured by the islanders he befriended and aided. Despite his best efforts, however, he made few converts to Christianity. It is said one of the primary reasons for this was his insistence on sexual abstinence prior to marriage and fidelity after.

Along the coastline, tiny villages are separated by long stretches of beach and brush. Accommodations are limited to guest houses and a couple of resorts (one very upscale) near the south end. An impressive wall borders the south end of the island, and most diving is done in this area. There are also some nice shallow reefs inside the wall and along the east and west coasts.

Cat Island Dive Sites

82 Dry Heads

Dry Heads is one of the prettiest and healthiest shallow reefs in The Bahamas. It derives its name from the fact that it is awash at low tide. The site features a relatively small primary reef area surrounded by sand flats and scattered smaller coral heads. The entire reeftop is carpeted with purple sea

Location: South of Alligator Point

Depth Range: Surface–23ft (7m)

Access: Boat or shore

Expertise Rating: Novice

Local children frolic at Dry Heads, one of The Bahamas' healthiest shallow reefs.

fans, and the corals are supremely healthy from top to bottom. From the surface, the reef drops to a sand boundary. The most-prolific hard corals here are the perfect star-coral mounds. Schools of pretty French grunts mill about the hard-coral bases and sides, while southern stingrays rest on the white-sand bottom. The smaller invertebrate life is astounding—the list reads like the index of a reef life ID book.

Dry Heads arguably stands head and shoulders above the best of the Bahamian shallow reefs. Be sure to put this on your list of must-do dives.

83 Greenwood Reef

This large reef area lies very close to shore, offering easy access. On the southeast side of Cat Island, immediately offshore from the Greenwood Resort, this extremely shallow reef is very good for casual snorkeling. Although the base

Location: Just west of Greenwood Resort, north of Columbus Point

Depth Range: 5-25ft (1.5-7.6m)

Access: Shore

Expertise Rating: Novice

Keep an eye out for reclusive seahorses.

of the reef is extinct, it exhibits excellent top growth, with elkhorn and fire corals predominating.

The fish life at Greenwood Reef is fairly good, tending toward friendly angelfish and butterflyfish. Rainbow wrasses are possible unusual inhabitants. The seagrass beds surrounding the reef shelter many wrasses and gobies. Look for seahorses and blackear wrasses and check the sand flats for various shellfish and razorfish, both rosy and pearly.

84 Black Coral Wall

Access to this impressive wall is subject to weather conditions, but the dive is spectacular on a good day. Spur-and-groove formations spill over the wall at 60 to 80ft. The grooves form sand chutes, while the spurs climb up to grow together, forming arches suitable for swimming through. The site gets its name from its larger-than-normal number of black coral stands, which are intertwined with wire corals.

Large pelagics frequent this corner of the island, but the main draw is the annual gathering of mating groupers. It is mostly tiger groupers that visit this site, arriving in December, often traveling great distances. The mating period

Location: West of Columbus Point

Depth Range: 50-130ft+ (15-40m+)

Access: Boat

Expertise Rating: Intermediate

lasts a short time, usually less than a week. Consider yourself fortunate if you're able to witness this gathering of thousands of groupers as few divers have actually seen it. Other spots where this natural phenomenon occurs include nearby Rum Cay, a meeting point for Nassau groupers.

85 The Cut

This simple shore dive will satisfy divers and snorkelers alike. The elkhorn and staghorn corals are surprisingly healthy for such an easily accessed site.

Location: Just offshore in Reef Harbour

Depth Range: 15-30ft (4.6-9.1m)

Access: Shore

Expertise Rating: Novice

Much of Cat Island's shore is rugged limestone.

After a simple swim out through an easy-to-spot break in the reef, you'll find separate sections of reef on both sides of this cut and spreading out into deeper water. Swim straight out less than 50 yards and you will find elkhorn corals in water slightly deeper than they normally are found. You'll notice that the elkhorns stretch up toward the surface, rather than branching out to the sides as they do in shallower water.

The night diving is excellent on this site due to the large numbers of crabs and lobsters along with other nocturnal creatures like red night shrimp. If you're fortunate, you'll spot a red-banded lobster.

86 Devil's Point

The wall drops very quickly in this section off Devil's Point. The drop-off exhibits excellent hard-coral growth. Soft corals proliferate on the wall's upper portion, while plate corals dominate the growth below 70ft. Large purple and yellow tube sponges, wire corals (one of the five forms of black coral) and deepwater sea fans add interest. The site's near-constant current attracts plenty of schooling fish. Large black groupers are very common.

Oddly, the southern walls of Cat Island have garnered surprisingly little recogni-

Location: Southeast of Devil's Point

Depth Range: 45-130ft+ (14-40m+)

Access: Boat

Expertise Rating: Advanced

tion among Bahamian divers and visitors. This makes little sense, as the sites are solid and can easily compete with any found in The Bahamas.

Stands of brilliant purple tube sponges are a staple of Bahamian diving.

87 Tartar Bank

Tartar Bank offers one of the finest and most challenging dives off Cat Island. An offshore pinnacle about three-quarters of a mile in diameter rises from nearly 2,000ft to just 40ft from the surface. The edge of the actual wall starts at 60 to 80ft, before plummeting into the deep.

Surprisingly, the hard-coral growth, though good, is not the site's dominant feature. The sponges and deepwater sea fans tend to be very large, but they are not the main attraction either. The real attraction at Tartar Bank is the site's exposed open-water position, which

Location: South of Devil's Point

Depth Range: 40-130ft+ (12-40m+)

Access: Boat

Expertise Rating: Advanced

draws large pelagics. Sightings of sharks, spotted eagle rays, turtles and amberjacks should be expected.

This dive demands advanced skills because of the strong currents often experienced here.

Long Island Group Dive Sites

Long Island is the southeasternmost of the Bahamian islands that offer both great diving and professional dive operators. With neighboring Conception Island and Rum Cay, the Long Island group offers a full spectrum of dive possibilities.

Columbus probably made his third landfall on Long Island, an event commemorated on the island's extreme north end with an pyramid perched on a white limestone cliff. Long Island also holds some of the few remnants of the islands' pre-Columbian inhabitants—painted walls and a few rare artifacts have been found in stalactite-rich caves to the south, near Deadman's Cay. At the south end of Exuma Sound, Long Island's northern tip is only about 25 miles (40km) from the southern islands of the Exumas chain. Long Island is so named because it stretches 66 miles (106km) but seldom reaches more than a few miles wide.

Long Island is as relaxed as any of the Out Islands. Days are consumed mainly with fishing and farming. Much farming is done in the unique approach of pothole farming—crops grow in the rich topsoil that collects in holes eroded in the limestone. The land ranges from marshland and rolling hills to strands of powder-soft beaches and sheer limestone cliffs buffeted by the crashing Atlantic.

Much of the diving is done on the patch reefs between northern Long Island and Great and Little Exuma, as well as around nearby Conception Island and Rum Cay.

Long Island Group Dive Sites	Good Snorkeling	Novice	Intermediate	Advanced
88 Shark Reef			●	
89 Sea Garden	●	●		
90 Flamingo Tongue	●	●		
91 Barracuda Heads	●	●		
92 MV *Comberbach*			●	
93 Poseidon Point	●	●		
94 Dean's Blue Hole & Big Green Hole			●	
95 Southampton Reef	●	●		
96 Conception Wall			●	
97 Snow Fields	●	●		
98 Chimney			●	

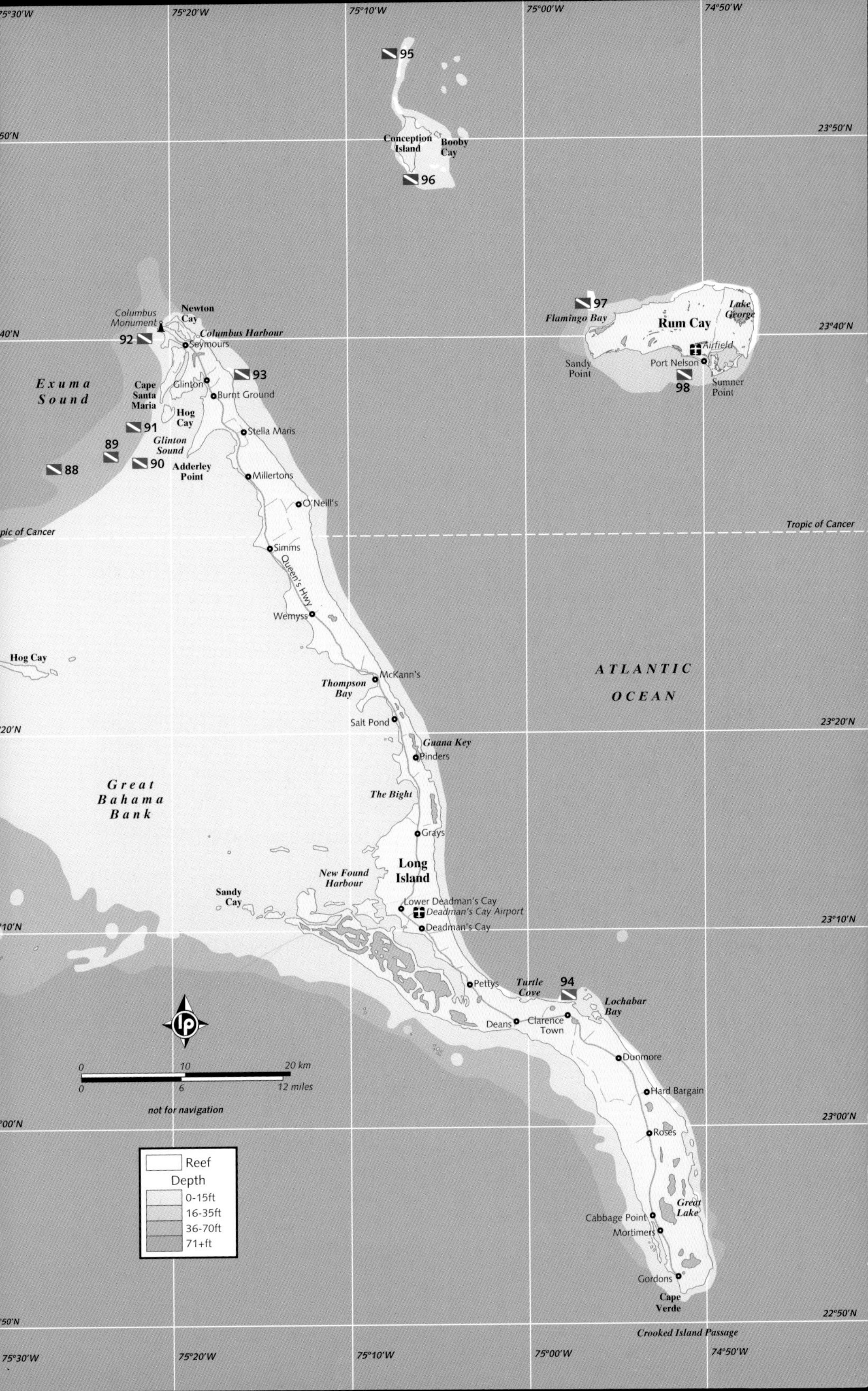

75°30'W   75°20'W   75°10'W   75°00'W   74°50'W

95

23°50'N

Conception Island   **Booby Cay**

96

97
Flamingo Bay   **Rum Cay**   *Lake George*

Newton Cay
Columbus Monument   *Columbus Harbour*   23°40'N
92   **Seymours**   **Airfield**   Port Nelson   **Sumner Point**
Sandy Point   98

Cape Santa Maria   Glinton   93   Burnt Ground
Hog Cay   91   Stella Maris
89   *Glinton Sound*
88   90   **Adderley Point**
Millertons

Exuma Sound

O'Neill's

Tropic of Cancer - *Tropic of Cancer*   23°30'N

Simms

Wemyss

ATLANTIC OCEAN

McKann's
Thompson Bay
Salt Pond   23°20'N
Guana Key
Pinders

Hog Cay

The Bight

Great Bahama Bank   Grays

Long Island

New Found Harbour
Sandy Cay   Lower Deadman's Cay
Deadman's Cay Airport   23°10'N
Deadman's Cay

Pettys   *Turtle Cove*   94
Deans   *Lochabar Bay*
Clarence Town
Dunmore   23°00'N

IP

0   10   20 km
0   6   12 miles
not for navigation

Hard Bargain

Roses

Great Lake

Cabbage Point
Mortimers

| Reef |
| Depth |
| 0-15ft |
| 16-35ft |
| 36-70ft |
| 71+ft |

Gordons
Cape Verde   22°50'N

Crooked Island Passage

75°30'W   75°20'W   75°10'W   75°00'W   74°50'W

88 Shark Reef

Bahamian shark diving started at Shark Reef. When the people from Stella Maris began doing this dive some 30 years ago, the prevailing opinion was they were flat-out crazy. In truth, they probably were somewhat crazy. At that point our understanding of in-water interactions with what were considered ferocious and unpredictable predators was limited. Shark diving was indeed bold, but it inspired other operators to follow suit, eventually turning The Bahamas into the shark-diving capital of the Caribbean.

The shark encounters take place on a large coral reef (300ft long and 200ft wide), which features high-profile coral heads, some of which rise 25ft from the bottom. The average depth is about 50ft.

The shark feed is done differently than most others in The Bahamas. The

Location: 7 miles (11km) northwest of Stella Maris Marina

Depth Range: 25-50ft (7.6-15m)

Access: Boat

Expertise Rating: Intermediate

predominant shark species at this site is the Caribbean reef shark. You'll see as many as two dozen at a time. Divers are arrayed on the bottom, then a bucket of chum is released from the stern of the vessel. After the frenzy of the feed, the sharks return to meandering around the reef.

Divers are free to explore the reef after the feed, making this a pleasing combination of an exhilarating shark dive and a satisfying reef dive—with toothy companions!

89 Sea Garden

Tall stands of pillar corals, beds of staghorn corals, groupers hiding within waving soft corals and clouds of blue

Location: West of Hog Cay

Depth Range: 15-25ft (4.6-7.6m)

Access: Boat

Expertise Rating: Novice

A curious Nassau grouper visits a coral head.

chromis—Sea Garden is a lovely little patch of isolated coral heads, each abuzz with activity. The corals are in very good shape here.

Though simple, Sea Garden is very exciting, with plenty to keep you going for several dives. With squirrelfish in every corner and bigeyes peering out of holes, it's a great place for macro-photography.

90 Flamingo Tongue

Flamingo Tongue is a little reef with a lot to offer. Named for the large number of flamingo tongue snails that feed on the abundant soft corals, the site also features numerous small coral patches. The reef has an angular profile, with overhangs and small caverns sheltering large numbers of reef fish. Large sea fans are just one prominent feature of this fine reef.

Location: Southwest of Calabash Bay

Depth Range: 20-35ft (6-11m)

Access: Boat or shore

Expertise Rating: Novice

Though the larger, deeper section of the reef is accessible only by boat, there is a nice shallow section that you can reach from shore. The shallow section is only a few feet deep and reaches to the surface in some places. Enter by walking across the limestone at the extreme southern end of the beach.

The waters around Long Island foster magnificent sea fans as much as 6ft across.

91 Barracuda Heads

A classic Long Island dive, Barracuda Heads is named for the abundance of great barracuda that make their home here. It has all the requisite elements for inclusion on the must-see dive menu. Large coral heads with many nooks and crannies create corners of interest. Clear,

Location: West of Hog Cay

Depth Range: 15-50ft (5-15m)

Access: Boat

Expertise Rating: Novice

Black coral grows just a quarter-inch per year.

calm waters contribute to the peaceful atmosphere.

Barracuda Heads is composed of about a half-dozen large coral heads that measure 50 to 60ft long and 30ft wide and rise 20 to 25ft from the seafloor. The heads are honeycombed and seem like fish-filled apartment complexes. The multitude of marine inhabitants allows hours of interesting observation. Tunicates, hydroids and soft corals jostle hard corals and anemones for living space. Resident Nassau, tiger, yellowfin and red groupers share dining privileges with the 'cudas, some of which reach the 30-to-50lb range. Black corals grow under protected ledges, sharing space with both spiny and slipper lobsters.

92 MV *Comberbach*

The MV *Comberbach*, a 102ft British freighter built in 1948, was scuttled in 1986 by the folks at Stella Maris to form an artificial reef for the pleasure of visiting divers. Fully prepared with the safety of divers in mind, the *Comberbach* has become nicely encrusted in the 15 years since she slipped beneath the waves.

You'll see all sorts of algae, sponges and corals. She sits upright, with her superstructure at 65ft and her keel at 100ft. A 1975 Ford van rests inside her

Location: North end of Calabash Bay

Depth Range: 65-100ft (20-30m)

Access: Boat

Expertise Rating: Intermediate

hold. Passengers of the vehicle include a number of large Nassau groupers and a fairly shy green moray.

Fishing with Frogfish

Frogfish, also known as anglerfish, are difficult to find because they look like lumpy sponges or pieces of coral. The longlure frogfish—the most common frogfish species on Caribbean reefs—relies on this camouflage to ambush its prey in a unique manner.

The fish's "lure" is a spine that extends from its head in front of its mouth. The spine, called an illicium, has a small piece of skin on the end that looks like a worm. When a passing fish tries to eat the bait—gulp!—it's swallowed whole by the frogfish, whose mouth extends forward to suck in its prey. Frogfish eat a wide variety of prey, and can consume fish as large as they are.

93 | Poseidon Point

You can drive right up to the entry point of this easily accessible reef site. The reef reaches within 25 yards of the rocky shore, so it only takes a short swim to get there.

The site is usually protected from poor weather conditions, but days with high winds from the east will rule out diving here.

Underwater, elkhorn corals share space with various types of finger corals and healthy staghorn corals. Sea fans sway in the gentle surge. There are lots of

Location: Off the Atlantic coast, 3 miles (4.8km) north of Stella Maris Marina

Depth Range: 5-35ft (1.5-11m)

Access: Shore

Expertise Rating: Novice

little tropicals to maintain your interest, and you will certainly see some larger groupers and stingrays.

94 Dean's Blue Hole & Big Green Hole

Two blue holes sit close together on the southeastern coast of Long Island near Clarence Town, one to the north and one to the south.

Dean's Blue Hole is both the deepest and the largest recorded blue hole found in The Bahamas to date. In August 1992, Jim King bottomed Deans out at 660ft—nearly twice the depth of the majority of the deepest recorded blue holes in The Bahamas. The hole is open to the ocean, with corals and fish occupying a steep slope at the mouth.

Big Green Hole is found in a shallow lagoon just inside the shoreline. The set-

Location: Near Clarence Town at Lochaber

Depth Range: Surface to 130ft+ (40m+)

Access: Shore

Expertise Rating: Intermediate

ting is very tranquil. It's a trek to get there, but it's worthwhile. This hole can only be penetrated to 66ft. The surrounding area offers excellent snorkeling.

Dean's Blue Hole is the largest and deepest blue hole as yet recorded in The Bahamas.

Snowy egrets frequent The Bahamas.

Conception Island

An uninhabited island about 15 miles (24km) northeast of Long Island, Conception Island is a national nature reserve. The island also serves as a nesting site for shorebirds, waterbirds and marine turtles. Underwater, Conception Island offers drop-dead gorgeous walls and lots of marine life.

95 Southampton Reef

This shallow reef has taken a good bit of punishment from hurricanes over the past decade, but it still holds plenty of potential. Southampton Reef is very long, stretching north from Conception Island's northwest corner.

The reef is home to a wreck usually called the No Name Wreck. The vessel is believed by some to be the remains of the HMS *Southampton*, a 32-gun English frigate that foundered on the reef on November 27, 1812. The wreck was initially located in 1970, by Joerg Friese of Stella Maris, as he flew low over the reef.

The vessel does appear to be from the early 19th century. Although there are

Location: North of Conception Island

Depth Range: 5-20ft (1.5-6m)

Access: Boat

Expertise Rating: Novice

no cannons—they would have been salvaged if at all possible—there are four anchors, three propellers, a pile of anchor chain, boilers, engine frame and other remnants of the ship. The remains are spread over an area 800ft long and 300ft wide.

96 Conception Wall

Conception Wall is the general name given to a number of separate sites along the wall south of Conception Island. The area offers excellent opportunities for both medium-depth and deep wall diving. The absolutely pristine reefs are representative of some of the finest diving this hemisphere has to offer. Access to this area is either by liveaboard dive vessels or through daytrips originating from Long Island.

Magnificent high-profile coral heads are interspersed with sand chutes spilling

Location: Southwest of Conception Island

Depth Range: 60-130ft+ (18-40m+)

Access: Boat

Expertise Rating: Intermediate

over the wall. The lush sides of the coral heads are solid masses of extremely healthy corals and volcano, elephant-ear, vase and barrel sponges. Schooling horse-eye jacks, snappers and solitary groupers give way as sharks wander the corridors between the coral heads. Turtles are sighted on almost every dive.

Conception Wall can stand with some of the best sites found in other great Caribbean destinations such as Cozumel or the Caymans. The topography of the reef and the adjacent wall is so perfect and healthy and the fish life so abundant that one would think it was created just for divers. Both the island and the marine environment are formally defined as national parkland and are protected by the Bahamas National Trust. This protection, in conjunction with the lack of human intrusion and development, is certainly the underlying factor supporting these pristine conditions.

The walls off Conception Island are as vibrant and beautiful as any in the Caribbean.

Rum Cay

Ten miles (16km) southeast of Conception Island lies Rum Cay, home to a population of about 100 souls. Rum Cay has been a stalwart Bahamian diving legend for decades. The island's best diving is found in protected areas to the south and to the northwest. As there is no functional dive operation on Rum Cay at present, these sites are reached only by live-aboards or long daytrips from San Salvador or Long Island. Given the common fluctuations of the Bahamian dive industry, this could change at any time.

97 Snow Fields

A large patch reef surrounded by white sand, Snow Fields is a fine reef for both snorkeling and shallow diving. The site is also great for macrophotography.

Location: 100 yards (91m) west of Rum Cay

Depth Range: 17-30ft (5.2-9.1m)

Access: Boat

Expertise Rating: Novice

There was a magnificent elkhorn coral field here, but it has been largely destroyed by a recent spate of hurricanes. This fast-growing coral will regenerate within several years, but for the moment, algae has taken over the many of the broken stumps. Despite the storm damage, hundreds of star and brain corals rise as much as 10ft off the bottom, providing shelter for coneys, groupers, butterflyfish and a large number of basslets.

A coney peeks out from between the arms of a sea rod.

98 Chimney

In this area, the top of the drop-off begins at 50ft. A 4ft-by-8ft hole in the top of the reef drops 40ft, emerging into a large grotto with a white-sand floor. Exit the grotto via a long, sandy ravine, following it until it spills out onto the vertical drop-off at 130ft, then follow the wall back up.

Location: Southeast of Port Nelson

Depth Range: 50-130ft+ (15-40m+)

Access: Boat

Expertise Rating: Intermediate

Giant sponges and clusters of gorgonians—primarily deepwater sea fans—are the rule. You'll also see plenty of large barrel sponges, wire corals and schooling horse-eye jacks.

San Salvador Dive Sites

Though disputed by some, San Salvador's claim to world fame is as Columbus' first landfall on his first voyage in 1492. For today's visitors San Salvador represents the ideal of life in the Out Islands. With a population of only about 700 people, San Sal sports a comfortable small-town atmosphere. The island has plenty of historical and natural features—there are sea caves etched into the shoreline and an inshore cave system, monuments to Columbus, one of the world's oldest operating kerosene light-houses, the ruins of Loyalist plantations and obscure remains of the area's original Amerindian inhabitants. The island also has plenty of those fine white-sand beaches for which The Bahamas is famous—most of them completely deserted.

Situated in the open ocean 575 miles (926km) southeast of Miami, San Salvador is geographically unusual for The Bahamas. While most Bahamian islands are joined to a shallow bank, San Salvador is the exposed peak of a subsea moun-tain. Only about six Bahamian islands share this distinction, all in the southeast.

As a result, San Salvador is surrounded by walls. The island is legendary for its wall diving. Divers in The Bahamas in the 1960s were among the pioneers of the over-the-wall experience. Off the western shore a massive submerged cliff hugs the shoreline and drops fast. By the time you're a mile offshore, you're in water a few thousand feet deep. When you reach 2 and 3 miles (3.2 and 4.8km) out, you're in water 6,000 to more than 10,000ft (1,800 to 3,000m) deep. Don't think this is all

San Salvador Dive Sites	Good Snorkeling	Novice	Intermediate	Advanced
99 SS *Frascate*	●	●		
100 Telephone Pole			●	
101 Snapshot Reef	●	●		
102 Devil's Claw			●	
103 Hole in the Wall			●	
104 North Pole Cave			●	
105 Great Cut			●	
106 Black Forest			●	
107 Double Caves			●	
108 French Bay			●	

deep diving, however. The walls start at just 40 to 50ft (12 and 15m), and there are some fine shallow snorkeling sites.

The enormous depths so close to shore mean there is a wealth of marine life. From a fascinating array of tiny critters to the usual varieties of reef fish, as well as hammerhead sharks, San Sal will keep you on your toes. Perhaps the most notable marine-life feature of San Salvador diving is the grouper population. Found at virtually every dive site, Nassau groupers are the unofficial ambassadors of San Salvador. They greet you as soon as you enter the water, tag along like puppies all through your dive and bid you farewell as you depart. Fish-feeding, once popular here, has ceased, but the groupers keep coming around.

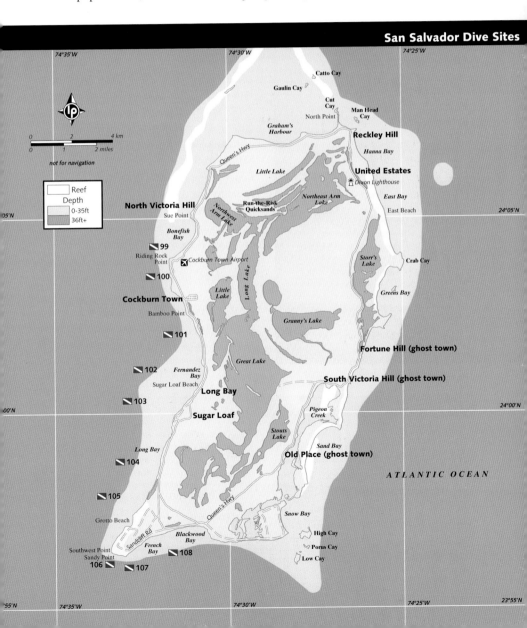

San Salvador Dive Sites

99 SS *Frascate*

The SS *Frascate* may be the best 20ft-deep shipwreck site in the Caribbean. Built in Germany in 1886 and originally named the *Daszig*, this 261ft vessel was acquired by a British firm, renamed and put into

Location: North of airport runway, off Riding Rock Point

Depth Range: 6-21ft (1.8-6.4m)

Access: Boat

Expertise Rating: Novice

Inside the *Frascate*'s massive boiler.

service hauling freight between the U.S. and the Caribbean.

She was en route from New York to Jamaica on a calm New Year's Day in 1902 when she went aground in just 20ft of water. Apparently, the crew had a little too much fun celebrating the night before. Considered a hazard to navigation, the *Frascate* was salvaged and blown apart by the Army Corps of Engineers during WWI.

Wreckage now blankets a large area of the sea bottom. Two huge intact boilers big enough to swim through lie on their sides, dominating the seascape. Other parts of the twisted wreckage make great compositional elements for wide-angle photography. There are always plenty of fish on the site, with groupers, eels, black durgon and queen triggerfish prevalent.

100 Telephone Pole

Marked by a telephone pole lying on the sandy bottom, this site is a San Sal classic. A pure white-sand bottom slopes from 35ft beneath the boat to a little more than 50ft where the reef borders the wall. If you pop up to the top of the reef, you'll be at 30ft. Move forward 15ft and you'll peer down the vertical face of the wall into the

Location: Off Bamboo Point

Depth Range: 30-130ft+ (9.1-40m+)

Access: Boat

Expertise Rating: Intermediate

cobalt blue of the abyss. A cleft nearly 20ft tall cuts straight through the reef—if you go through it, you'll emerge on the wall at 80ft.

Groupers love this site. They meet you right at the boat and escort you around the reef. They're so friendly that they can become downright annoying. The wall has lots of rope and tube sponges, along with orange elephant-ear sponges.

This site, along with much of the nearby wall, is plagued by seasonal algal overgrowth. The growth tends to be most prevalent in the warmest months, but all it takes is one good fall storm to clear it away. In any case, the algae honestly does not detract significantly from the dive experience.

Groupers welcome you on nearly every San Sal dive.

101 Snapshot Reef

There is a good chance that more published photos of little marine critters have been taken at this one reef than from any other single dive site in the world, thus the name. Some of the earliest organized underwater photography classes in The Bahamas were conducted here with Paul Tzimoulis, the longtime publisher of *Skin Diver* magazine. Dedicated searches for suitable subjects and intensive photo examination allowed novice underwater photographers a number of excellent opportunities.

Put on your magnifying glasses and look close—the many nooks and crannies of this low-lying reef create perfect hiding places for all sorts of invertebrates

Location: Southwest of Bamboo Point

Depth Range: 10-20ft (3-6m)

Access: Boat

Expertise Rating: Novice

and smaller fish. Look for flamingo tongues and the much rarer fingerprint cyphoma, yellow stingrays, various anemones, yellow goatfish and mutton snappers.

Though the corals are not as healthy here as at other sites, the marine life more than makes up for it.

102 Devil's Claw

Beginning at 45ft atop the wall, three deep crevices cut into the face of the wall to 85ft. It looks as if some demonic creature raked its three-fingered claw down the wall, gouging out this trio of deep scrapes, earning the site its name—Devil's Claw.

Devil's Claw is an impressive site, not just for the topography, but also for the variety of marine life. A sloping wall drops down to a small plateau with plate and star corals at 85ft. Below this it plunges into the depths. Look for black

Location: West of Long Bay

Depth Range: 45-130ft+ (14-40m+)

Access: Boat

Expertise Rating: Intermediate

coral trees at about 90ft. Groupers, barracuda, grunts and crabs are common, while king mackerel, tuna, sharks and rays make periodic appearances.

103 Hole in the Wall

At this site, rolling mounds of coral begin at 40ft, drop to 65ft and then climb back to the edge of the wall at 45ft, before dropping at a severe angle. Two cuts in

Location: Off Sugar Loaf Beach

Depth Range: 40-130ft+ (12-40m+)

Access: Boat

Expertise Rating: Intermediate

the wall—the north cut is the longer and deeper of the pair—join at the edge of the wall at 90ft, forming a Y. Immediately in front of the ravines you'll find a large coral ridge broken off the main wall—its top at 70ft and its base at 150ft. Just south of the coral ridge, a very large, wide cut starts at 50ft, with ridges dropping past 130ft. The peak of this cut features a 7ft stand of pillar coral.

Plenty of sponge formations adorn this portion of the wall—look for of rope sponges and large elephant-ear sponges, as well as stands of black corals. Keep an eye on the blue water for schools of horse-eye jacks, crevalle jacks, sharks, eagle rays and the rare manta ray.

A brilliant sponge attracts a diver's attention.

104 North Pole Cave

A sand bottom drops to 50ft, where it meets the coral ridge on the edge of the wall. This ridge climbs to between 30 and 35ft, before sloping back to 50ft and then beginning a more severe drop. An opening at 70ft leads to a chimney, which emerges on the wall's vertical face at 110 to 130ft. Be cautious of your depth, as the topography of the site can be deceptive.

Bermuda chubs are seen in the midwater. The face of the wall is dressed

Location: Northeast of Southwest Point

Depth Range: 30-130ft+ (9.1-40m+)

Access: Boat

Expertise Rating: Intermediate

up in sheets of star corals and large stovepipe and barrel sponges.

105 Great Cut

Great Cut is an extremely unusual formation and a truly spectacular site. At some point in the distant past, a cataclysmic event caused a 200ft-long section of the wall to split from the main wall, creating a double drop-off. The sand bottom of the island's shelf slopes down to 55ft, where it meets a coral ridge. The ridge runs parallel to the shore and crests at 35ft. As you pass over the crest of this ridge, you will find yourself floating over a chasm that drops to 150ft. Cross this gap to reach the second section of the wall—it peaks at 80ft and falls absolutely vertically into the depths.

The entire area is rich with a variety of corals. Large black coral trees and purple tube sponges protrude from the wall. A short tunnel cuts through the second portion of the wall, opening onto the outer face of the wall. Emerge from this cave and you will find yourself floating in the deep blue. Groupers in the 20-to-40lb range are common and fearless.

Location: North of Southwest Point

Depth Range: 35-130ft+ (11-40m+)

Access: Boat

Expertise Rating: Intermediate

A bull lobster stands its ground at the peak of Great Cut.

106 Black Forest

Black Forest is a good example of the standard San Salvador profile—a sand flat dropping to 60ft, a ridge climbing up to 35ft and then a slow drop into the deep

Location: Southwest of Sandy Point

Depth Range: 35-130ft+ (11-40m+)

Access: Boat

Expertise Rating: Intermediate

A belted cardinalfish rests among coral polyps.

blue. Cracks and crevices penetrate the reef, creating overhangs that shelter large groupers and snappers. One of the crevices is overgrown, turning into a tunnel that opens onto the wall at 100ft.

This is a very rich area for a tremendous variety of hard corals. Pillar corals are plentiful in the shallows, while thick clusters of black corals hang off the wall, lending the site its name. Turtles seem to be more abundant here than elsewhere, and as always in the southern sector, watch for great hammerheads and spotted eagle rays.

107 Double Caves

Double Caves is much more than just a pair of caves cutting through the reef. It is the beginning of the extreme spur-and-groove formations spilling over the edge of the wall that typify the southern side of underwater San Salvador.

At the edge of the sand plain at 55ft, the reef builds up to 35ft, then drops vertically to a steep slope at 165ft. Two primary caves begin at 60ft in the sand plain on the inside of the wall. These deep crevices overgrown with corals penetrate the body of the wall at 80ft and emerge on the face of the wall at 110ft.

In addition to the two primary caves, there are a number of deep crevices where

Location: West French Bay, near Sandy Point

Depth Range: 35-130ft+ (11-40m+)

Access: Boat

Expertise Rating: Intermediate

the spurs have grown into walls. In some places these spurs grow together, forming arches and swim-throughs. Watch for sharks coming in from the open waters. Hammerheads in particular are common to this area.

108 French Bay

French Bay is not a single dive site. Instead, it's an entire area with more than a dozen named sites that share several common elements. The actual topography differs from site to site, but shared traits include an extremely variegated reef face and walls that begin in 35 to 50ft before plunging precipitously.

Location: Southeast of Blackwood Bay

Depth Range: 30-130ft+ (9.1-40m+)

Access: Boat

Expertise Rating: Intermediate

In this area the wall is exposed to extremely deep waters, offering a treasure trove of large marine life. The reef itself is a classic spur-and-groove formation, with sand chutes spilling over the wall and extremely high reef structures. The spurs join together in places, forming arches that emerge onto the wall.

One of the biggest attractions in French Bay is the presence of hammerhead sharks. Great hammerheads in the 12-to-16ft range are encountered regularly year-round. A more-unusual phenomena in The Bahamas is the annual gathering of scalloped hammerheads. The scalloped hammerheads usually show up in the late summer and early fall. Groups range from just a few to four dozen or more.

The Undiscovered Bahamas

Tucked away in the extreme southeastern corner of The Bahamas are a number of "undiscovered" islands and cays that hide diving treasures. These far-flung spots are beyond the reach of the casual traveler and untouched by dive operators. A few day boats make occasional forays to the less-distant islands, while the others are visited by live-aboards when weather conditions permit. The future of diving in The Bahamas can be found in the undisturbed marine environments around these isolated islands. Among the possibilities are:

Hosgsty Reef: Perhaps the least visited of the group, this is the Atlantic Ocean's only true atoll—it's a horseshoe-shaped reef lying just off two tiny sand spits. Highlights include deep walls, giant sponges, and a freighter grounded in the reef.

Inagua Islands: Great Inagua is home to some 50,000 West Indian flamingoes. Once seen throughout the archipelago, they are now seldom seen in the wild outside of the Inaguas. Salt is also harvested commercially here—the bird's nesting habits have been incorporated into the production process in a complex, ecologically sensitive system. Diving highlights include several wrecks and dramatic walls, while Little Inagua offers some promising shallow sites.

Samana Cay: Surrounded by fringing reefs and precipitous walls, this uninhabited cay is a primary launching point for expeditions in search of migrating humpback whales.

Plana Cays: These uninhabited cays are a refuge for The Bahamas' only endemic mammal, the hutia, a rodent similar to a guinea pig. The islands are the flat tops of column-like pinnacles as deep and steep as any wall in the country.

Mayaguana: Divers can enjoy plenty of extensive fringing reefs and walls starting in only 20ft (6.1m).

Marine Life

The Bahamas' variety of fish and invertebrate species will satisfy the most ardent fish-watcher or photographer. A wealth of shallow reefs and the generally accepted practice of non-interference with life on the reef allows a close approach by the quiet diver. Many of the species in The Bahamas are pan-Caribbean—few species are limited to The Bahamas. With luck you'll spot pelagics such as sea turtles, manta and eagle rays, dolphinsfish, marlins, swordfish and whale sharks. The following gallery includes images of fish and invertebrates you are likely to encounter in Bahamian waters, along with their common and scientific names. Following this you will find photos and details about potentially dangerous animals you may encounter in Bahamian waters.

Common names are used freely but are notoriously inaccurate and inconsistent. The two-part scientific name, usually shown in italics, is more precise. It is made up of a genus name followed by a species name. A genus is a group of closely related species that share common features. A species is a recognizable group within a genus whose members are capable of interbreeding. Where the species or genus is unknown, the naming reverts to the next known level: family (F), order (O), class (C) or phylum (Ph).

Common Vertebrates

French angelfish
Pomacanthus paru

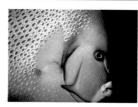

gray angelfish
Pomacanthus arcuatus

queen angelfish
Holacanthus ciliaris

fairy basslet
Gramma loreto

banded butterflyfish
Chaetodon striatus

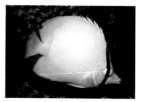

spotfin butterflyfish
Chaetodon ocellatus

coney
Epinephelus fulvus

yellowtail damselfish
Microspathodon chrysurus

slender filefish
Monacanthus tuckerii

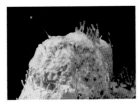

longlure frogfish
Antennarius multiocellatus

spotted goatfish
Psuedupeneus maculatus

sharknose goby
Gobiosoma evelynae

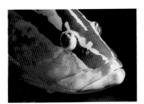

Nassau grouper
Epinephelus striatus

French grunt
Haemulon flavolineatum

red hind
Epinephelus guttatus

bar jack
Caranx ruber

yellowhead jawfish
Opistagnathus aurifrons

sharpnose puffer
Canthigaster rostrata

sand diver
Synodus intermedius

schoolmaster
Lutjanus apodus

glasseye snapper
Priancanthus cruentatus

yellowtail snapper
Ocyurus chrysurus

squirrelfish
Holocentrus ascensionis

trumpetfish
Aulostomus maculatus

Common Invertebrates

sponge brittle star
Ophiothrix suensonii

queen conch
Strombus gigas

orange cup coral
Tubastrea coccinea

rose lace coral
Stylaster roseus

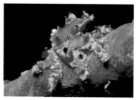
cryptic teardrop crab
Pelia mutica

swimming crinoid
Analcidometra armata

rough fileclam
Lima scabra

flamingo tongue
Cyphoma gibbosum

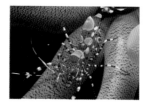
spotted cleaning shrimp
Periclemenes yucatanicus

squat anemone shrimp
Thor amboinensis

Caribbean reef squid
Sepioteuthis sepiodea

Christmas tree worm
Spirobranchus giganteus

Hazardous Marine Life

Marine animals almost never attack divers, but many have defensive and offensive weaponry that can be triggered if they feel threatened or annoyed. The ability to recognize hazardous creatures is a valuable asset in avoiding accident and injury. The following are some of the potentially hazardous creatures most commonly found in The Bahamas.

Barracuda

Barracuda are identifiable by their long, silver, cylindrical bodies and razorlike teeth protruding from an underslung jaw. They swim alone or in small groups, continually opening and closing their mouths, an action that looks daunting but actually assists their respiration. Though barracuda will hover near divers to observe, they are really somewhat shy, though they may be attracted by shiny objects that resemble fishing lures. Irrigate a barracuda bite with fresh water, and treat with antiseptics, anti-tetanus and antibiotics.

Fire Coral

Although often mistaken for stony coral, fire coral is a hydroid colony that secretes a hard, calcareous skeleton. Fire coral grows in many different shapes, often encrusting or taking the form of a variety of reef structures. It is usually identifiable by its tan, mustard or brown color and fingerlike columns with whitish tips. The entire colony is covered by tiny pores and fine, hairlike projections nearly invisible to the unaided eye. Fire coral "stings" by discharging small, specialized cells called nematocysts. Contact causes a burning sensation that lasts for several minutes and may produce red welts on the skin. Do not rub the area, as you will only spread the stinging particles. Cortisone cream can reduce the inflammation, and antihistamine cream is good for killing the pain. Serious stings should be treated by a doctor.

Moray Eel

Distinguished by their long, thick, snakelike bodies and tapered heads, moray eels come in a variety of colors and patterns. Don't feed them or put your hand in a dark hole—eels have the unfortunate combination of sharp teeth and poor eyesight, and will bite if threatened. If you

161

are bitten, don't try to pull your hand away suddenly—the teeth slant backward and are extraordinarily sharp. Let the eel release it and then surface slowly. Treat with antiseptics, anti-tetanus and antibiotics.

Lesser Electric Ray

Electric rays can be found hovering over sand patches or partially buried in the sand. They have a rounded flat body that is blue-gray on top with a light underbelly. Unique electrical organs composed of muscle tissue lie on either side of the body disc and are filled with cells much like electrical plates in a battery. The shock of electric rays found in The Bahamas is not strong enough to seriously injure a diver, but the discharge is powerful enough to get your attention and make you wish you had turned the other way.

Scorpionfish

Scorpionfish are well-camouflaged creatures that have poisonous spines along their dorsal fins. They are often difficult to spot since they typically rest quietly on the bottom or on coral, looking more like rocks. Practice good buoyancy control, and watch where you put your hands. Scorpionfish wounds can be excruciating. To treat a puncture, wash the wound and immerse it in nonscalding hot water for 30 to 90 minutes.

Sea Urchin

Sea urchins tend to live in shallow areas near shore and come out of their shelters

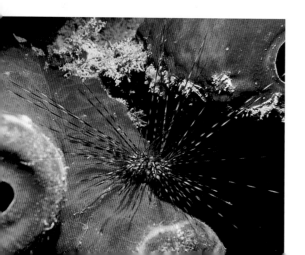

at night. They vary in coloration and size, with spines ranging from short and blunt to long and needle-sharp. The spines are the urchin's most dangerous weapon, easily able to penetrate neoprene wetsuits, booties and gloves. Treat minor punctures by extracting the spines and immersing the area in nonscalding hot water. More serious injuries require medical attention.

Shark

Sharks come in many shapes and sizes. They are most recognizable by their triangular dorsal fin. Though many species are shy, there are occasional attacks. About 25 species worldwide are considered dangerous to humans. Sharks will generally not attack unless provoked, so don't taunt, tease or feed

them. Avoid spearfishing, carrying fish baits or mimicking a wounded fish, and your likelihood of being attacked will greatly diminish. Face and quietly watch any shark that is acting aggressively and be prepared to push it away with a camera, knife or tank. If someone is bitten by a shark, stop the bleeding, reassure the patient, treat for shock and seek immediate medical aid.

Southern Stingray

Identified by its diamond-shaped body and wide "wings," the stingray has one or two venomous spines at the base of its tail. Stingrays like shallow waters and tend to rest on silty or sandy bottoms, often burying themselves in the sand. Often only

the eyes, gill slits and tail are visible. These creatures are harmless unless you sit or step on them. Though injuries are uncommon, wounds are always extremely painful, and often deep and infective. Immerse wound in nonscalding hot water and seek medical aid.

Bristle Worm

Also called fire worms, bristle worms can be found on most reefs. They have segmented bodies covered with either tufts or bundles of sensory hairs that extend

in tiny, sharp, detachable bristles. If you touch one, the tiny stinging bristles lodge in your skin and cause a burning sensation that may be followed by a red spot or welt. Remove embedded bristles with adhesive tape, rubber cement or a commercial facial peel. Apply a decontaminant such as vinegar, rubbing alcohol or dilute ammonia.

Diving Conservation & Awareness

As a nation built largely on the wealth of its marine resources, The Bahamas has developed a strong sensitivity to the preservation of its environment. Historically, conservation efforts have been tempered by the needs of a developing nation. In recent decades, however, the fight has taken many positive steps. Today numerous official nature preserves—covering a total of 238,000 acres (96,315 hectares)—protect both land and marine areas under the auspices of the Bahamas National Trust.

The Bahamas Diving Association (BDA) self-imposes strict rules regarding marine conservation and diver safety for its members. Permanent moorings, mostly of the conservation-minded Halas design, have been placed at the vast majority of dive sites to accommodate day boats as well as live-aboards.

Dive operators take environmentalism very seriously, with all operators enforcing a "no-take, no-touch" policy. The main exception to this rule is the common practice of taking lobsters and conchs from permitted areas on longer excursions. Bahamian law forbids the use of scuba while lobstering and conching—they may be taken by free-divers only. Lobstering has been a major problem in the past, especially the practice of bleaching—squirting chlorine bleach into the reef to force lobsters out. Bleaching is now outlawed, as it damages the corals.

Long-lining for sharks was another problem during the early years of shark feeds, but public outcry forced the government to realize that the value of the Bahamian shark population as a tourism resource far outweighed the needs of a small fishing industry based on a fragile species.

Responsible Diving

Dive sites tend to be located where the reefs and walls display the most beautiful corals and sponges. It only takes a moment—an inadvertently placed hand or knee, or a careless brush or kick with a fin—to destroy this fragile, living part of our delicate ecosystem. By following certain basic guidelines while diving, you can help preserve the ecology and beauty of the reefs:

1. Never drop boat anchors onto a coral reef and take care not to ground boats on coral. Encourage dive operators and regulatory bodies in their efforts to establish permanent moorings at appropriate dive sites.

2. Practice and maintain proper buoyancy control and avoid over-weighting. Be aware that buoyancy can change over the period of an extended trip. Initially you may breathe harder and need more weighting; a few days later you may breathe

more easily and need less weight. Tip: Use your weight belt and tank position to maintain a horizontal position—raise them to elevate your feet, lower them to elevate your upper body. Also be careful about buoyancy loss: as you go deeper, your wetsuit compresses, as does the air in your BC.

3. Avoid touching living marine organisms with your body and equipment. Polyps can be damaged by even the gentlest contact. Never stand on or touch living coral. The use of gloves is no longer recommended: gloves make it too easy to hold on to the reef. The abrasion caused by gloves may be even more damaging to the reef than your hands are. If you must hold on to the reef, touch only exposed rock or dead coral.

4. Take great care in underwater caves. Spend as little time within them as possible, as your air bubbles can damage the fragile organisms. Divers should take turns inspecting the interiors of small caves or under ledges to lessen the chances of damaging contact.

5. Be conscious of your fins. Even without contact, the surge from heavy fin strokes near the reef can do damage. Avoid full-leg kicks when diving close to the bottom and when leaving a photo scene. When you inadvertently kick something, stop kicking! It seems obvious, but some divers either panic or are totally oblivious when they bump something. When treading

The ecologically sensitive Halas mooring.

water in shallow reef areas, take care not to kick up clouds of sand. Settling sand can smother the delicate reef organisms.

6. Secure gauges, computer consoles and the octopus regulator so they're not dangling—they are like miniature wrecking balls to a reef.

7. When swimming in strong currents, be extra careful about leg kicks and handholds.

8. Photographers should take extra precautions, as cameras and equipment affect buoyancy. Changing f-stops, framing a subject and maintaining position for a photo often conspire to prohibit the ideal "no-touch" approach on a reef. When you must use "holdfasts," choose them intelligently (i.e., use one finger only for leverage off an area of dead coral).

9. Resist the temptation to collect or buy coral or shells. Aside from the ecological damage, taking home marine souvenirs depletes the beauty of a site and spoils other divers' enjoyment.

10. Ensure that you take home all your trash and any litter you may find as well. Plastics in particular pose a serious threat to marine life.

11. Resist the temptation to feed fish. You may disturb their normal eating habits, encourage aggressive behavior or feed them food that is detrimental to their health.

12. Minimize your disturbance of marine animals. Don't ride on the backs of turtles or manta rays, as this can cause them great anxiety.

Marine Conservation Organizations

Coral reefs and oceans are facing unprecedented environmental pressures. The following groups are actively involved in promoting responsible diving practices, publicizing environmental marine threats, and lobbying for better policies.

CORAL: The Coral Reef Alliance
☎ 510-848-0110
www.coral.org

Ocean Futures
☎ 805-899-8899
www.oceanfutures.com

Cousteau Society
☎ 757-523-9335
www.cousteausociety.org

ReefKeeper International
☎ 305-358-4600
www.reefkeeper.org

Project AWARE Foundation
☎ 714-540-0251
www.projectaware.org

Listings

Telephone Calls

To call The Bahamas from the U.S., Canada or the Caribbean, dial 1 + 242 + the local seven-digit number. From elsewhere dial your country's international access code + 242 + the local number. Toll-free (800 or 888) numbers can be accessed from the U.S. and, usually, Canada.

Diving Services

The following dive operators are members of the Bahamas Dive Association (BDA). The BDA imposes a set of standards, so members exhibit a high level of professionalism. Other operators come and go—they vary in service quality but also open up new diving, often in territory not yet fully explored. Divers can get a complete listing of dive services from the Bahamas Tourist Board. The operators listed below are divided by island.

New Providence

Bahama Divers Ltd.
P.O. Box 5004
East Bay St., Nassau
☎ 393-5644/6054 fax: 393-6078
U.S. ☎ 954-351-9750
toll-free ☎ 800-398-3483
bahdivers@divers.com
Sales: Yes **Rentals:** Yes
Boats: Two 42ft custom dive boats
Trips: 2-tank morning; 1-tank afternoon; dedicated snorkeling trips
Classes: PADI 5-Star Facility; Open Water to Divemaster
Special Services: Manufacturer of Bahama Pro equipment

Custom Aquatics Ltd.
P.O. Box CB-12730
Coral Harbour, Nassau
☎ 362-1492 fax: 362-2045
young@grouper.batelnet.bs
Sales: No **Rentals:** Yes
Boats: 28ft Parker; 35ft Viking
Trips: Custom trips by appointment only
Classes: PADI; Open Water to Divemaster, specialties

Dive Dive Dive
P.O. Box N-8050
Coral Harbour, Nassau
☎ 362-1401 fax: 362-1994
toll-free ☎ 800-368-3483
info@divedivedive.com
www.divedivedive.com
Sales: No **Rentals:** Yes
Boats: 42ft Defender; 40ft Burns & Stillman
Trips: 2-tank morning; 2-tank afternoon; shark dives; technical dives
Classes: PADI, NAUI, SSI, NASDS, YMCA, TDI, ANDI; Open Water to Divemaster, specialties, technical training
Special Services: Nitrox

Diver's Haven
1 Marina Dr.
Paradise Island, Nassau
☎ 363-6716/363-3000 x6158
fax: 363-4401
info@divershaven.com
www.divershaven.com
Sales: Yes **Rentals:** Yes
Boats: Two 51ft Defenders; 55ft Defender; 50ft custom dive boat
Trips: 2-tank morning; 1-tank afternoon; custom and night dives on request
Classes: PADI, NAUI, NASDS, SSI; Open Water to Divemaster, specialties

New Providence (continued)

Nassau Scuba Centre
P.O. Box CB-11863
Coral Harbour, Nassau
☎ 362-1964 fax: 362-1198
U.S. ☎ 954-462-3400 fax: 954-462-4100
toll-free ☎ 800-327-8150
divr@divenassau.com
www.divenassau.com
Sales: Yes **Rentals:** Yes
Boats: 42ft Burpee; 42ft Newton; 30ft Leo;
55ft custom catamaran (for snorkeling &
scuba intro)
Trips: 2-tank morning; 2-tank afternoon;
shark dives
Classes: PADI, SSI; Open Water to
Instructor, specialties, shark feeder program
Special Services: Nitrox; multilingual staff

Stuart Cove's Dive Bahamas
P.O. Box CB-13137, Nassau
☎ 362-4171 fax: 352-5227
1045 SE 17th St.
Ft. Lauderdale, FL 33316, USA
U.S. ☎ 954-524-5755 fax: 954-524-5925
toll-free ☎ 800-879-9832
info@stuartcove.com
www.stuartcove.com
Sales: Yes **Rentals:** Yes
Boats: Three 40ft Michael Fitz; 40ft Maine
Down Easter; 54ft flattop; 43ft converted
sportfishing vessel; 32ft open V-hull; 50ft
custom dive boat
Trips: 2-tank morning; 1-tank afternoon;
snorkeling trips; trips to Exuma & Andros;
night dives; shark dives; submersibles; DPVs
Classes: PADI, SSI, NAUI, YMCA, NASDS;
Open Water to Instructor, specialties, shark
feeder program
Special Services: Nitrox; multilingual staff

Grand Bahama

**Club Fortuna/Viva Diving Undersea
Adventures**
P.O. Box F-42398
Churchill Rd. at Doubloon Dr., Freeport
☎ 373-4000 fax: 373-5555
U.S. ☎ 954-462-3400 fax: 954-462-4100
toll-free ☎ 877-564-8482
viva@nealwatson.com/vivadive@batelnet.bs
www.nealwatson.com
Sales: No **Rentals:** Yes
Boat: 28ft open-hull catamaran
Trips: 2-tank morning; 2-tank afternoon;
shark dives
Classes: PADI Openwater to Divemaster

Grand Bahama Scuba
P.O. Box F-42809, Freeport
☎ 373-6775/373-9791 fax: 373-9792
4631 NW 31st Ave., PMB #317356
Ft. Lauderdale, FL 33309, USA
toll-free ☎ 800-753-7282
fred@grandbahamascuba.com
www.grandbahamascuba.com
Sales: Yes **Rentals:** Yes
Boats: 30ft Island Hopper; 28ft Delta
Trips: 2-tank morning; 1-tank afternoon;
night dives on request; shark dives; cavern
dives
Classes: PADI, NAUI, SSI, IDA, TDI; Open
Water to Instructor, specialties
Special Services: Nitrox

Sunn Odyssey Divers
P.O. Box 44166, Freeport
☎ 373-4014 fax: 373-2629
sunnody@batelnet.bs
www.sunnodysseydivers.com
Sales: Yes **Rentals:** Yes
Boats: 32ft Island Hopper; 25ft Delta
Trips: 2-tank morning; 2-tank afternoon;
night dives on request
Classes: PADI, YMCA, SDI; Open Water,
specialties
Special Services: Nitrox

UNEXSO
Port Lucaya
☎ 373-1244 fax: 373-8956
P.O. Box 220687
West Palm Beach, FL 33422
U.S. ☎ 954-351-9889 fax: 954-351-9740
toll-free ☎ 800-992-3483
info@unexso.com
www.unexso.com
Sales: Yes **Rentals:** Yes
Boats: Two 30ft Island Hoppers; 42ft
Thomas; 45ft Michael Fitz; 40ft V-hull
Trips: Revolving dive schedule of 1-tank
dives (maximum 4 dives per day); night
dives; shark dives; dolphin encounters
Classes: PADI, NAUI, SSI; Open Water to
Rescue Diver, specialties, shark feeder pro-
gram, Dolphin Assistant Trainer Program

Grand Bahama (continued)

Xanadu Undersea Adventures
P.O. Box F-40118, Freeport
☎ 352-3811 fax: 352-4731
1525 S Andrews Ave.
Ft. Lauderdale, FL 33316, USA
U.S. ☎ 954-462-3400 fax: 954-462-4100
toll-free ☎ 800-327-8150
divexua@grouper.batelnet.bs
www.xanadudive.com
Sales: Yes **Rentals:** Yes

Boats: 37ft Islander; 40ft Adventure I; 52ft Adventure II
Trips: 2-tank morning; 1-tank afternoon; night dives on request; custom West End trips; shark dives; blue hole dives
Classes: PADI, IANTD; Open Water to Divemaster, specialties, technical and deep diving, shark feeder program, shark awareness classes
Special Services: Nitrox

Bimini

Bimini Undersea
Alice Town
☎ 347-3089 fax: 347-3079
P.O. Box 693515
Miami, FL 33269, USA
U.S. ☎ 305-652-9048 fax: 305-653-5572
toll-free ☎ 800-348-4644
info@biminiundersea.com
www.biminiundersea.com
Sales: No **Rentals:** Yes
Boats: 48ft Stapleton; 36ft V-hull
Trips: 2-tank morning; 1-tank afternoon; night dives; wild dolphin trips
Classes: PADI, NAUI, NASDS, SSI, YMCA, CMAS; Open Water, specialties

Scuba Bimini
P.O. Box 66, South Bimini
☎ 347-4444 fax: 347-4511
U.S. ☎ 954-524-6090 fax: 954-524-2145
toll-free ☎ 800-848-4073
info@scubabimini.com
www.scubabimini.com
Sales: No **Rentals:** Yes
Boats: 30ft Delta; 30ft Island Hopper; 30ft Uniflite
Trips: 2-tank dives; 1-tank dives; night dives; shark dives
Classes: PADI, NAUI, SSI; Open Water to Divemaster, specialties
Special Services: Nitrox

Abacos

Abaco Beach Resort Dive Centre
P.O. Box AB-20857
Marsh Harbour, Abaco
☎ 367-4646
toll-free ☎ 800-838-4189
info@abacodive.com
www.abacodive.com
Sales: No **Rentals:** Yes
Boat: 38ft custom dive boat
Trips: 2-tank morning; 1-tank afternoon (minimum 4 divers); night dives on request (minimum 4 divers)
Classes: PADI, NAUI, YMCA, CMAS, NASDS; Open Water to Divemaster, specialties

Brendals Dive Center
Green Turtle Cay, Abaco
☎/fax: 365-4411
U.S. ☎ 305-438-4222 fax: 305-438-2200
toll-free ☎ 800-780-9941

www.brendal.com
brendal@oii.net
Sales: Yes **Rentals:** Yes
Boats: 34ft Island Hopper; 29ft flattop
Trips: 2-tank morning; 1-tank afternoon; specialty adventure trips; night dives on request
Classes: PADI, NAUI, SSI; Open Water to Assistant Instructor

Froggies Out Island Adventures
Hope Town, Abaco
☎ 366-0431 fax: 365-6494
froggies@mail.batelnet.bs
www.oii.net/froggies/index.html
Sales: No **Rentals:** Yes
Boats: 55ft Defender; 35ft Lorquin; 35ft V-hull
Trips: 2-tank excursions with casual late departure; all-day dive/snorkeling beach excursions; night dives on request
Classes: PADI; Open Water to Rescue Diver

Abacos (continued)

Keith's Dive Abaco
P.O. Box 20555, Marsh Harbour, Abaco
☎ 367-2787 fax: 367-4779
toll-free ☎ 800-247-5338
dive@dive-abaco.com
www.dive-abaco.com
Sales: No **Rentals:** Yes
Boats: 30ft Island Hopper; 28ft Delta
Trips: 2-tank morning; 1-tank afternoon;
night dives on request; shark dives
Classes: PADI, NAUI, YMCA, CMAS; Open
Water to Divemaster, specialties

Sea Below Diving
Walker's Cay Hotel, Walker's Cay

☎ 353-1252 fax: 353-1252
700 SE 34th St.
Ft. Lauderdale, FL 33315, USA
toll-free ☎ 800-327-8150
U.S. ☎ 954-462-3400 fax: 954-462-4100
shkrodeo@batelnet.bs
www.walkerscay.com
Sales: Yes **Rentals:** Yes
Boats: 45ft Burpee; 42ft custom jet drive;
35ft Maine Coaster
Trips: 1- and 2-tank morning; night dives
Classes: PADI, YMCA, SSI, NAUI, PDIC,
CMAS; Open Water to Advanced
Special Services: Shark dives and shark
awareness classes; fishing excursions

Andros

Andros Undersea Adventures
Fresh Creek
☎ 368-2795 fax: 368-2796
toll-free ☎ 800-327-8150
AndrosMM@aol.com
www.divebahamas.com
Sales: No **Rentals:** Yes
Boat: 38ft Key West #1
Trips: 2-tank morning; 1-tank afternoon;
night dives; blue hole dives; deep dives
Classes: PADI; Open Water to Advanced,
specialties

Seascape Inn
P.O. Box 023824, Mangrove Cay, Andros
☎/fax: 369-0342
U.S. fax: 208-330-7293
relax@seascapeinn.com
www.seascapeinn.com
Sales: No **Rentals:** Yes
Boat: 34ft motorized catamaran
Trips: 2-tank morning; 1-tank afternoon;
night dives by request
Classes: PADI; specialties

Small Hope Bay Lodge
Fresh Creek
☎ 368-2014 fax: 368-2015
P.O. Box 21667
Ft. Lauderdale, FL 33335-1667, USA
toll-free ☎ 800-223-6961
shbmkt@smallhope.com
www.smallhope.com
Sales: No **Rentals:** Yes
Boats: 28ft tri-pontoon flattop; 36ft
tri-pontoon flattop; two custom V-hulls
Trips: 2-tank morning; 1-tank afternoon;
specialty trips on request; snorkeling; night
dives; technical dives; cave dives; deep
explorations; shark dives
Classes: PADI, TDI, SDI, YMCA, PDIC,
IANTD, NASDS, NSS, NAUI; Open Water to
Advanced, specialties, cave diving certification, deep diving certification
Special Services: Nitrox

Eleuthera

Ocean Fox Diving
Harbour Island Club & Marina
☎ 333-2323
Sales: No **Rentals:** Yes
Boats: 31ft Cat Limbo; 34ft Crusader
Trips: Custom trips, small groups
Classes: PADI; Open Water
Special Services: Deep-sea fishing trips

Valentine's Dive Center
P.O. Box 1, Harbour Island

☎/fax: 333-2080
dive@valentinesdive.com
www.valentinesdive.com
Sales: Yes **Rentals:** Yes
Boats: Two 32ft Island Hoppers
Trips: 2-tank morning; 1-tank afternoon;
custom charters; snorkeling excursions; night
dives; blue hole trips; DPV trips
Classes: PADI; Open Water to Advanced,
specialties

Exumas

ExumaSCUBA Aventures
Club Peace & Plenty
P.O. Box 29055
George Town, Exuma
☎ 336-2093 fax: 336-2093
toll-free ☎ 800-874-7213/800-525-2210
info@exumascuba.com
www.exumascuba.com
Sales: No **Rentals:** Yes
Boats: 26ft Bertram; 34ft pontoon for
snorkeling
Trips: 2-tank morning; 1-tank afternoon;
dedicated snorkeling trips; night dives on
request; blue hole trips
Classes: PADI; Open Water, specialties

Exuma Dive Centre
P.O. Box EX-29102
George Town, Exuma
☎ 336-2390 fax: 336-2391
toll-free ☎ 800-874-7213
exumadive@bahamasvg.com
Sales: No **Rentals:** Yes
Boats: Three boats
Trips: 2-tank morning; 1-tank afternoon;
dedicated snorkeling trips; night dives on
request; blue hole trips
Classes: PADI, IDA, NAUI; Open Water to
Divemaster, specialties

Cat Island

Cat Island Dive Center
Greenwood Beach Resort
Port Howe, Cat Island
☎/fax: 342-3053
toll-free ☎ 877-328-7475
gbr@grouper.batelnet.bs
www.greenwoodbeachresort.com

Sales: No **Rentals:** Yes
Boats: 30ft T-craft; 26ft ChrisCraft
Trips: 2- or 3-tank outings with late
departure; night dives by request
Classes: PADI; Open Water to Divemaster,
specialties

Long Island

Stella Maris Inn
☎ 338-2051/2053 fax: 338-2052
1100 Lee Wagener Blvd., Suite 354
Ft. Lauderdale, FL 33315, USA
☎ 954-359-8236 fax: 954-359-8238
toll-free ☎ 800-426-0466
smrc@stellamarisresort.com
www.stellamarisresort.com
Sales: No **Rentals:** Yes
Boats: 28ft Enterprise; 32ft Stapleton; 65ft
custom Norseman
Trips: 3-tank all-day trips; Conception Island,
Rum Cay, San Salvador custom overnights
on request; night dives on request
Classes: PADI, SSI; Open Water, specialties

Cape Santa Maria Beach Resort
Cape Santa Maria, Long Island
☎ 338-5273 fax: 338-6013
1327 Beach Dr.
Victoria, BC, Canada V8S 2N4
Canada ☎ 250-598-3366 fax: 250-598-1361
toll-free ☎ 800-663-7090
obmg@pinc.com
www.capesantamaria.com
Sales: No **Rentals:** Yes
Boats: 38ft Bertram; 31ft Bertram
Trips: 2-tank morning; 1-tank afternoon;
night dives on request; shark dives
Classes: PADI; Open Water, specialties

San Salvador

Riding Rock Inn
San Salvador
☎ 331-2631 fax: 331-2020
1170 Lee Wagener Blvd., Suite 103
Ft. Lauderdale, FL 33315-3561, USA
U.S. ☎ 954-359-8353 fax: 954-359-8254
toll-free ☎ 800-272-1492
info@ridingrock.com

www.ridingrock.com
Sales: No **Rentals:** Yes
Boats: Two 40ft V-hulls; 40ft Hatteras
Trips: 2-tank morning; 1-tank afternoon;
night dives
Classes: PADI; Open Water to Divemaster,
specialties

Live-Aboards

The following is a list of live-aboards serving The Bahamas. These vessels depart from Miami, Fort Lauderdale and West Palm Beach (on the Florida coast), as well as from within The Bahamas (usually from Nassau).

Aqua Cat Cruises
102ft catamaran: *Aqua Cat*
P.O. Box 66-1658
Miami, FL 33266, USA
☎ 305-888-3002 fax: 305-885-3323
toll-free ☎ 888-327-9600
info@aquacatcruises.com
www.aquacatcruises.com

Blackbeard's Cruises
Three 65ft monohull sailboats: *Sea Explorer,
Morning Star, Pirate's Lady*
65ft luxury sailing catamaran: *CatPpalu*
P.O. Box 66-1091
Miami, FL 33266, USA
☎ 305-888-1226 fax: 305-884-4214
toll-free ☎ 800-327-9600
sales@blackbeard-cruises.com
www.blackbeard-cruises.com

Bottom Time Adventures
80ft motorized catamaran: *Bottom Time II*
P.O. Box 11919
Ft. Lauderdale, FL 33339-1919, USA
☎ 954-921-7798 fax: 954-920-5578
toll-free ☎ 800-234-8464
info@bottomtimeadventures.com
www.bottomadventures.com

Nekton Diving Cruises
Two 78ft SWATH vessels: *Nekton Pilot,
Nekton Rorqual*
520 SE 32nd St.
Ft. Lauderdale, FL 33316, USA

☎ 954-463-9324 fax: 954-463-8938
toll-free ☎ 800-899-6753
info@nektoncruises.com
www.nektoncruises.com

Ocean Explorer Charters
55ft specialized film-production yacht:
MV *Ocean Explorer*
65ft sailing catamaran: *Legacy* (operated by
Legacy Adventures)
14 S Via Lucindia
Stuart, FL 34996-6410, USA
☎ 561-288-4262 fax: 561-288-0183
toll-free ☎ 800-338-9383
info@oceanexplorerinc.com
www.oceanexplorerinc.com

Out Island Oceanics
65ft ocean cruiser: *Sea Dragon*
717 SW Coconut Dr.
Ft. Lauderdale, FL 33315, USA
☎ 954-522-0161 fax: 954-522-5939
seadragonbahamas@hotmail.com
www.seadragonbahamas.com

Sea Fever Diving Cruises
90ft converted oil-field crew boat: *Sea Fever*
1413 Great Neck Rd.
Virginia Beach, VA 23454, USA
☎ 305-531-6404 fax: 757-481-2075
toll-free ☎ 800-443-3837
seafever@seafever.com
www.seafever.com

Tourist Offices

Bahamas Ministry of Tourism
New Providence (Bahamas Main Office)
P.O. Box N-3701
Market Plaza, Bay St., Nassau
☎ 322-7500 fax: 328-0945
toll-free ☎ 800-866-3483
tourism@bahamas.com
www.bahamas.com

Miami (U.S. Main Office)
1 Turnberry Pl.,
19495 Biscayne Blvd., Suite 242
Aventura, FL 33180
☎ 305-932-0051 fax: 305-682-8758

Index

dive sites covered in this book appear in **bold** type

Lonely Planet Pisces Books

The **Diving & Snorkeling** guides cover top destinations worldwide. Beautifully illustrated with full-color photos throughout, the series explores the best diving and snorkeling areas and prepares divers for what to expect when they get there. Each site is described in detail, with information on suggested ability levels, depth, visibility and, of course, marine life. There's basic topside information as well for each destination.

Also check out dive guides to:

Australia's Great Barrier Reef	Cocos Island	Pacific Northwest	Southern California
Australia: Southeast Coast	Curaçao	Papua New Guinea	Tahiti & French Polynesia
Bali & Lombok	Florida Keys	Red Sea	Texas
Bermuda	Guam & Yap	Roatan & Honduras' Bay Islands	Thailand
Bonaire	Jamaica	Scotland	Turks & Caicos
Chuuk Lagoon, Pohnpei & Kosrae	Monterey Peninsula & Northern California	Seychelles	Vanuatu